The Pleasure
of Their Company

OTHER NONFICTION BOOKS BY
Doris Grumbach

The Presence of Absence:
On Prayers and an Epiphany

Life in a Day

Fifty Days of Solitude

Extra Innings: A Memoir

Coming into the End Zone: A Memoir

The Company She Kept

The
Pleasure
of
Their
Company

DORIS GRUMBACH

BEACON PRESS

BOSTON

B
Grum
C. 1

BEACON PRESS
25 Beacon Street
Boston, Massachusetts 02108-2892
www.beacon.org

BEACON PRESS BOOKS
are published under the auspices of
the Unitarian Universalist Association of Congregations.

Printed in the United States of America
05 04 03 02 01 00   8 7 6 5 4 3 2 1

This book is printed on acid-free paper that meets the uncoated paper
ANSI/NISO specifications for permanence as revised in 1992.

Text design by Anne Chalmers
Composition by Wilsted & Taylor Publishing Services

Library of Congress Cataloging-in-Publication Data
Grumbach, Doris.
The pleasure of their company / Doris Grumbach.
p.   cm.
ISBN 0-8070-7222-2 (acid-free paper)
1. Grumbach, Doris.   2. Grumbach, Doris—Friends and associates.
3. Novelists, American—20th century—Biography.
4. Maine—Social life and customs.   I. Title.
PS3557.R83 Z476 2000
813'.54—dc21
[B]   99-053100

for

HANNAH YAROWSKY —

the youngest life of the party

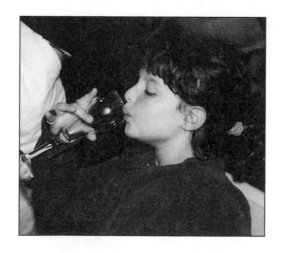

The living and the dead: I miss them all.
—Leon Wieseltier, *Kaddish*

We must fight old age as we would a disease.
—The aged Cato

I hear it as it was now and as it is then.
—Wallace Stegner, *Angle of Repose*

The Pleasure
of Their Company

I PLANNED A party in July. I would be eighty. I had never had
a large party before. I would look back to find friends to invite.
My address book had their names, but a few of them were no
longer here.

♦

ONE GROWS old, and the people one loved have died and,
strangely, taken on vitality in contrast to the living. The sad
part of having old friends is that they are gone long before you
are ready to have them leave. But still, they remained, leeches
on the memory, suddenly coming alive to me when I least expected them. They appear by involuntary memory, never
through an act of will, certainly not of reason. Effort could not
bring them back. Yesterday, because it was her birthday, I remembered that Maggie would be one hundred if she had lived.

I see Margaret Schlauch as she was sixty years ago, a whiz at
languages and an always-smiling-as-she-lectures professor of
the history of the English language, Geoffrey Chaucer, medieval literature, seated on a bench in the zocalo in Mexico City
reading a Spanish newspaper aloud to me, me, the dullard-at-

acquiring-languages student of seventeen. I was so slow at learning Spanish that she had adopted this oral method to accustom my ear to the sounds. We had been in Havana for a month, in Mexico for two weeks, and she, who knew hardly a word of the language when we sailed on the *Morro Castle* (later to sink tragically) from New York, now spoke fluently and had no trouble reading the paper.

"Why does it come so quickly to you, and so slowly to me?" I remember asking her.

"Well, it grows easier the more languages one knows, I suppose."

"How many do you know?"

"About fifteen, I think," she said, putting down the newspaper. She opened a slim pamphlet that contained lists of words in Nahuatl, the language of the Aztecs. She came to Mexico to begin constructing the first Nahuatl grammar.

"Oh well," I thought as I opened my beginner's Spanish grammar and began to work on verb tenses.

Maggie was my guide (I think the correct current terms are "mentor" or "role model," but I dislike them both), as well as my friend and teacher. She made medieval literature so compelling as a scholarly endeavor that I changed my undergraduate major from philosophy to English (to Sidney Hook's disgust who assured me Professor Schlauch was not "a thinker"). In 1952 when she refused to take the loyalty oath required of college teachers at that time (she was a member of the then-legal Communist Party, I believe), she went to Poland to live and establish the department of English philology at the University of Warsaw.

Did she know Polish when she left? I doubt it but still, in the bibliography that appeared in a Festschrift to her published in 1971, there is listed a scholarly article on Chaucer's *Troilus and*

Cressida written in Polish less than two years after her arrival in Warsaw.

We stayed in touch by means of her serious publications and my very slight novels in the early sixties. Always, hers came inscribed and one of mine was dedicated to her. Oddly, she stepped far outside her scholarly medieval world in 1969 to review for the *Southern Review* two books on the poetry of meditation. At the top of the offprint of it she sent to me she wrote: "A strange subject for a life-long non-believer, don't you think? They asked me for it. I must have a former student on that magazine."

One year I received a little treatise, "The Doctrine of Vera Nobilitas as Developed after Chaucer," which was inscribed: "With Chaucerian Greetings." She noted that initials were often like names, of persons, i.e., indicative of their occupations. She said that the Germans talk of *Namenzwang* (Dr. Footer the podiatrist, de Gaulle the warrior). Our initials might be called *Initialszwang*, hers (MS) for her lifelong work on manuscripts, mine (DIG) because "you have learned to dig the younger generation."

During one of her semester visits to this country (on a diplomatic passport), she spent a day at the college in Albany at which I taught, talking about the commonality of languages (I believe I was the only person there who had ever heard of the illustrious scholar before, so the attendance was very sparse). Another time I went to visit her at the University of Connecticut, where she was teaching. We talked for hours about her life abroad (she was reticent about whether she had found there what she had gone to find, true equality and opportunity for all people) and my humdrum domestic life here. After that we lost touch.

In 1979 I asked the Polish cultural attaché (who was spending a day at the Villa Serbeloni in Bellagio, where I was work-ing) if he was acquainted with Professor Schlauch, if he knew how she was, and if he would carry an unsealed letter to her upon his return. He said he did, he thought she was well, and he promised to deliver it. I never heard from her again. She seemed to have slipped silently into that vast behind-the-iron-curtain territory from which we rarely had news. At the last I read a brief obituary in the *New York Times* that told me noth-ing except the usual facts of her birth, education, publications, and death.

It is a truism that one must have some sort of "closure" to be at peace with the death of a beloved. I have learned that to me the absence of closure is preferable. Without it, the dead exist somewhere, out of time and place, in permanent residence in my memory. So Maggie lives on in a remote corner of Para-guay, hard at work on the acquisition of a new language and planning a grammar of it for the Guayaki Indians.

◆

A FEW WEEKS later, it would have been Kay Boyle's ninety-fifth birthday. She has been dead for fifteen years. In my acute memory of her, she is sitting in a sunlit, meticulously furnished room in her Haight-Ashbury townhouse, dressed and coifed elegantly, her face crossed with deep lines, her prominent nose rising aristocratically beneath her high white forehead, and in her lobes the large white earrings she has worn in one form or another every day of her adult life.

She told me once about participating in a Vietnam peace demonstration in San Francisco and burning the draft cards of young men on the steps of the federal courthouse so that she would be arrested, not they. She supported the protest of black students at San Francisco State College, where she taught in her seventies. Everything about her erect, elegant person ran counter to the cliché of the young, disheveled, often violent radical. Her tired eyes lit up as she described the asservating events.

In my mind, still seated on her Victorian sofa in her tasteful living room, she is planning to go to Washington to protest the signing of the welfare bill by the president, or his betrayal of his gay and lesbian supporters in the military by making wrong-headed demands on them, or angrily on the telephone to her senator to object to the pointless, wag-the-dog bombings of sites in the Balkans, or to protest the injustices that are being perpetrated against the poor, the homeless, the sick, the wrongly imprisoned, the conscientious objectors.

◆

BARBARA PROBST, who died this summer, was my friend in *Mademoiselle* days in the early forties, when that women's magazine was young and vigorous. She and I were in awe of the notable persons who would come by to see George Davis, the fiction editor who had published one excellent novel, *The Opening of a Door*. Gypsy Rose Lee, the famous stripteaser, came regularly to visit him in his minuscule office at lunchtime. Novelist Carson McCullers would take him off for drinks at the Russian Tea Room at four. Sometimes Wystan Hugh Auden and his friend Christopher Isherwood would wait in the reception room to take him to dinner.

Probst and I had no part in this parade of celebrity. I was a proofreader. She was responsible for getting the publication out on time. She was smart, vigorous, reliable, and possessed of a dream that one day she would have a bookstore as far from

New York City as she could get. Almost sixty years later she succumbed to a multiplicity of illnesses to which she was always good-humoredly resigned.

Probst was born in Florida to a military family, I believe, and sent away to a girls' camp in her early teens. Together with her serge bloomers, middy blouses, and Keds, she insisted on taking with her a gift from her father, a small cannon. Years later she still had it when she sold her manual typewriter for a small part of the down payment on a farm in upstate New York that she converted into a bookstore, turning the pigpen into an annex to the huge barn. In that small outbuilding I found a book by Ellen Terry, the actress friend of Bernard Shaw, on an unexpected subject, the ballet. Probst sold it to me for a dollar. Later I discovered it was worth many times that. Then I knew it was a gift.

I remember she was the first person I knew to own a riding lawn mower. I see her astride it still, reducing the lawns she had created on the farm to green perfection. The bookstore, named the Owl Pen (why, I do not know), was on a dirt road off a dirt road (her description), and very difficult to find, a problem she added to by placing a very few signs at crossroads, signs so small they were easy to overlook. Customers brought their lunch with them when they planned a visit, taking into account the time it would take to get lost, find the place, browse, buy, have their picnic on the lawn, then turn around and get lost again.

After Probst was no longer able to run the store, even with the help of Jean, her companion of many years, she retired to a small house nearby (the road she lived on had a splendid view of the Vermont hills). She maintained her lifelong affection for cigarettes and whiskey, studied the stock market, and invested. The last time we saw her, in June of her eighty-third year, she had oxygen as constant companion for her emphysema. But she blithely ignored its presence and was still smoking.

We brought her a present, a bottle of Canadian Club. She was having trouble standing erect and breathing. Osteoporosis had shrunk her, but she smiled broadly when we came and expressed delight at the appropriateness of the gift. . . . I am certain she is now seated in the book-lined pigpen, smoking and sipping whiskey, her hand resting on the gray shank of her beloved little cannon.

◆

THERE WAS Dorothy Day, one of the few true Christians I was fortunate enough to have encountered in my lifetime. Halfway through college, and moved by guilt for my well-to-do bourgeois life in contrast to the hard-pressed, proletarian students at the city university we attended, I learned about Dorothy's house for the homeless and hungry on Mott Street, a brownstone, as I recall, deep in the slums of what was then called Little Italy. The house was within walking distance of Washington Square. The Depression was at its nadir; a line of hungry people wound down the street from where she and others served vegetable soup, bread, and coffee every day.

On the two days I had free of morning classes I helped out in the kitchen, often washing dishes with Dorothy, who lived at the house. I remember once noticing that her arms were covered with red marks, which, she explained to me, came from bedbugs, a phenomenon that I had never encountered on West End Avenue.

My admiration for that incredible woman was unending. Years later, I went on a retreat with her at Graymoor, New York. By then she was bent and gray and very thin. She held my arm as we walked about the grounds of the retreat house and talked about her life as if it were the best anyone could imagine, without any worldly possessions or pleasures except the knowledge that she had obeyed the God she loved and who, she believed, had showered her with ineffable benefits and love.

Recently there has been a move by a Catholic cardinal in New York to have Dorothy Day sanctified. Her response to such a suggestion, made often in her lifetime, was: "Don't call me a saint—I don't want to be dismissed that easily."

For me, Dorothy still lives as she had always lived, without a halo, handing out doughnuts and coffee on some celestial breadline, smiling at the women and men she serves, and scratching at the red lumps on her arms. For surely, if Heaven is as all-inclusive as it is rumored to be, there is room for bedbugs there.

◆

INEXPLICABLY, UNEXPECTEDLY, May Sarton left a hole in my life when she died four years ago at the age of eighty-three. I knew her for twenty-five years, after she responded to a review I wrote of one of her novels in the *New Republic*. I admired her persistence and skill in projecting a noble, unselfish, solitude-loving, generous, and warmhearted public persona, entirely unlike her true self, to an ever-increasing public who adored her and associated their own humdrum, often lonely, mostly female persons with her artfully manufactured fictional portrait.

In her last years she was cared for by an unusual woman, Susan Sherman, who had begun an association with May by writing her master's thesis on her work, and then went on to extraordinary acts of self-sacrifice in order to shore up May's insatiable need for company, applause, and uncritical approval.

Sherman was known to have driven on a snowy Sunday morning from her home north of New York city to the house in York, Maine (surely more than five hours), in very bad weather to bring May her Sunday *New York Times*. She then turned right around and drove back to New York in order to be on time for her teaching job the next morning.

Usually, Sherman's car was filled with a dozen fresh roses when she arrived at May's door. Her days and nights were concerned solely with May's letters, which she edited (there has been one selected volume published, and three others including a volume of letters to Juliette Huxley, I have been told, are to come). She has culled from May's work an extensive book of tidbits, and researched assiduously all the minutiae of biography and literary allusion mentioned anywhere in May's journals, letters, and writings.

So dedicated was Sherman to her subject that, when last I spoke to her, she was collecting every book *mentioned* by May in her books. And I have been told that, on May 3, a year after May's death, she visited her grave in Nelson, New Hampshire, met a couple who were similarly engaged, and asked them to join a "grieving society" that she was forming.

Sherman knew the real, solipsistic May Sarton well, but still, she spent and, for all I know, is still spending much of her life serving the carefully created image. What greater devotion to a fiction can there be? As for me, I have always thought of May primarily as a "character," someone so complex and colorful that she might be useful in a novel. I got as far as to conceive of such a work, to be written from a surviving devotee's point of view, and to be called *The Spinster's Widow*. It is very likely that I shall never write it. But I rather liked the title.

Both the character and the "real" May have survived in my memory, after she had been cremated and her ashes placed in the small plot in Nelson. That day was raw and wet. Leaves swirled around us in a wild wind, and an even heavier storm threatened. I stood with Margot Peters, her biographer, and pulled my coat around me against the sharp, cold wind, thinking: of course, May Sarton would not have missed this. She is here, in one of her temperamental outbursts, bringing about this weather. Or perhaps she is demonstrating her displeasure at my presence: her friend S.S. had not invited me to the small ceremony for a dozen people, but I had come anyway.

◆

A RECENT LOSS was a marvelous woman named Luree Miller who died young, in her early seventies, of the same cancer that had earlier afflicted her husband, Bill. She was a knowledgeable traveler; she wrote very well about women travelers in the last century. She was one of those persons who could be indignant with grace; in her book about her mother's slow decline into senility, she excoriated the medical establishment and nursing home facilities for their insufficient care of the aged.

I find it hard to accept the fact of her premature (to my mind) departure. It is easier to remember the beautiful bench she donated to a small park on Capitol Hill in Washington, to the back of which she had affixed a bronze tablet in memory of her husband. It was stolen once, but the anger of the community at the irreverent act was so great that the guilty neighbor returned it. Then Luree had it chained to the ground. I have not been back to see it, but it must be there still, and, as surely, she is forever seated on it, smiling happily in the wan Capitol sunshine, and watching the neighborhood children playing on the nearby rocks.

◆

I MISS THEM all, all gone over the divide from our temporary, insufficient, present existence.

O death, where is thy sting?

Everywhere.

◆

AGAINST ALL reason I decided to buy a new car, a Toyota Camry, recommended by my daughter and *Consumer Reports.* The Subaru, often called Maine's official car, had aged with me. A seven-year-old car is equivalent to a very elderly owner in wear and tear on its propulsive appendages and the state of health of its innards, its body rust, dents, creaks, and groans.

I went through all the usual absurdities with the Toyota salesman, putting up with his many trips "to check with the manager" about my offer of my car plus a firm amount of cash. Finally we came to terms, my terms. I gave him the title and keys to the Subaru, wrote a check, and drove away in an almost-new car (it had been leased for fifteen thousand miles by a seemingly neat and careful driver), thinking as I went: this is the height of incredibly foolish optimism—an eighty-year-old woman buying a new car.

◆

TO LIGHTEN my day I thumbed through *This Literary Life,* by Peter Van Straaten, a slim volume of very funny cartoons. A wife sits beside her fat, exhausted husband on the sofa and says: "If you've finished writing your trilogy, would you please take out the trash?" It always brought to mind the day one of my young daughters asked me: "Why don't you stop typing and bake a cake?"

◆

M<small>Y</small> LONGTIME project for the summer was to reread Proust, this time in the reworked (that is, not wholly changed) version by Terence Kilmartin of C. K. Scott-Moncrieff's famous translation, and stemming from the French edition published by Pleiade rather than the earlier Gallimard one. My intention was to read it slowly, stopping often for some contemporary fiction. I chose Don DeLillo's new novel, *Underworld*. I was pleased to discover that, like Proust, DeLillo observed a curious progress of events: "It was all falling indelibly into the past," he writes, as though what one hides in memory is still there forever, waiting to be rediscovered.

Indelibly? Is memory an unerasable bank, with nothing altered, nothing omitted by the judgments of time and revised by faulty recall? Is nothing added along the way during the many occasions of retrieval and narrative? Nothing censored by regret or guilt?

Michael Wood wrote a good review of *Underworld* and said: "We can't erase it [the past], but it will never be anything but the past." Yet when Proust evokes a past event by the reoccurrence of a sensory experience it becomes more than that, a new and present matter. The past is expanded and becomes a better thing. This happens in the imagination, in fiction, after the remembrance of things past, but not in life. The past more often diminishes and then blots out the present.

Early in February I began to worry about the party in July. When I reached eighty I presumed it would be my last. I could not avoid the feeling that it had to be as good a shindig as I was capable of devising.

I thought of friends, old ones reaching back to my young womanhood who should be on the list of people I wanted to be there. But I did not invite them. Some, like Gilbert Harrison, the respected owner and editor of *The New Republic* in my days there, were aged like me and lived too far away or were too ill to make the trip. Abigail McCarthy had recently fallen down a flight of stairs and hurt herself badly. Edward Crohn was now a distant, Christmas-card-only contact; once we had been close friends. He is the son of a father so famous that the disease he discovered was named for him, and, in his own right, is a retired physician whose talents have been in the service of veterans at a hospital in Buffalo. For one reason or another, they would not be there.

A few contemporaries would be able to attend. Helen Yglesias lives a few miles away in summer. She is a friend of ten years in Maine. Oddly, we had both grown up in New York City at the same time and later worked at parallel jobs—she was literary editor of the *Nation* and I of *The New Republic*, but we had never met until I looked her up in Maine. The Falks would be there, bookseller-comrades my partner, Sybil, and I knew from the time of our arrival here. Except for them, I realized, all the invitees would be younger, indeed, considerably younger than I.

I had entered what others have called the unfamiliar, foreign country of old age. In a letter used by Richard Ellmann as an epigraph in his fine biography of Oscar Wilde, I had found an even better metaphor for it:

> I . . . wish we could talk over the many prisons of life—prisons of stone, prisons of passion, prisons of intellect, prisons of morality and the rest—all limitations, external or internal, all prisons, really. All life is a limitation.

Prison is a useful image for old age. Oscar Wilde, who died at forty-five, did not live to enter it. In his stark definition, prison is synonymous with limitation. Old age is both the final limitation and the ultimate prison. From it there is no chance for escape or improvement. It is beyond pardon or commutation, it is the last sentence, it is the period to the sentence of change.

Nonetheless, I decided to have a celebration, as if these dire bounds did not exist, as if hope of some small future was still a thing with feathers. If it is true, and it is, that the daily newspaper in the country of age consists mainly of obituaries, I will try, for that weekend, to ignore them and read the funnies, *Hagar* and *The Wizard of Id* and *Dilbert* and *Doonesbury* and *Sally Forth*. I will try to do what Malcolm Cowley (in *The View from Eighty*) urged upon old people: display an "obstinate refusal to surrender in the face of time."

◆

MY GRANDDAUGHTERS decided that what I needed for my birthday was a pet. They themselves have always had two huge dogs, a black Lab and a golden retriever, as well as a crazy, elderly cat who dislikes people and cherishes her solitude in the basement. They wanted to give me a puppy. I explained my inability to care for a puppy. I described the dangers of falling on ice while walking the pet and of the nearby road if it ran free. But I promised I would think about a pet.

I did. I decided I would acquire a year-old, spayed, declawed, short-haired gray cat in time for the arrival of the little girls at the party. It had to be a tame, settled animal, not driven by the need to destroy the furniture or pee in the closet. It would not shed, so what I believed to be my lifelong allergy to cats would not be affected.

I watched the ads in the local newspaper for just such an animal and told the postmistress, dispenser of all the news in our community of about seventy-five persons and herself the owner of a beautiful cat, of my search. One morning in mid-May she called to tell me there was a kitten there I might like to see. Sybil and I went over to the small room that is our post office, five minutes from the house by car, and found a kitten, seated sedately in the office window, her white paws together, her Elizabethan white ruff shining, her small, seductively cocked head with all the markings of a common tabby cat, her outsized tail looking slightly Persian, and her hair very long. She had the blue eyes of an immature kitten. She was from a litter of six.

"How old is she?" we asked her owner.

"Six weeks. One thing: she won't use the litter box if it's not clean."

I looked at the kitten again. She cocked her head to the other side as if she were debating her choice of me as prospective owner.

"I'll take her," I said and gathered up the yellowish, long-haired, unspayed, immature kitten and carried her to the car. After much debate I named her Kitty Kelley after an acquaintance in Washington who writes biographies of famous persons and had, when I knew her, blonde hair and blue eyes. I called my granddaughters and assured them I now possessed a pet.

Often I have wondered why I feel this compulsion to record an event as insignificant as the acquisition of a cat. Three persons have since said to me that they were certain I would not be able to resist writing about Kelley. I vowed I would not do so, having read numberless (and mostly boring) accounts of people's cats; in fact, I think cat books constitute a whole shelf in Sybil's bookstore across our yard.

But then, by accident, I found in an old notebook a reference to what Nigel Nicolson reported of Virginia Woolf's reasons for keeping a diary and writing letters. "Nothing really happens until you have described it," she said. Nicolson believed Woolf had committed suicide because "she thought she had lost the gift of writing, and what was the purpose of life if she could not describe it?"

Woolf was in agreement with John Ruskin, who wrote: "The greatest thing a human soul ever does in this world is to see something, and to tell what it saw in a plain way. . . . To see clearly is poetry, philosophy and religion all in one." And I suppose, if I were presumptuous, I would add: "to tell it plainly is good writing."

So, in order to legitimize Kitty Kelley's existence I put her down on paper.

But as I did, I remembered something contrary to Woolf's and Ruskin's view. Thomas Merton wrote in his fifth journal: "What matters most is secret, not said. This begins to be the most real and most certain dimension."

What now?

◆

An old theological difficulty attempts to collate the existence of God with the presence of evil and suffering in the world. St. Theresa of Avila had a witty way of expressing it. She believed deeply in God but reproved Him for His behavior. "You have few friends because you treat them so badly."

◆

My literary judgment, which I once prized beyond reason, was no longer simply a matter of taste, honed discernment, or the result of wide reading. No, a new and curious element had entered into it: age, and its accompanying ill, poor vision. Someone sent me a new novel that is printed in what I took to be six-point Obscurant, a typeface I invented to explain my dislike of the book, not to describe the contents but the size of the type. What was even worse, the space between the words was uneven and thus almost illegible. Taken out of the hands of the fine-press printer and relegated to machine setting, the appearance of the page was unpleasant, affecting my critical judgment, I feared.

The appearance of a book is no longer allowed to contribute to the success of its contents. To the contrary, a good book often gets very little aesthetic assistance from its housing.

So, either I needed to ignore the existence of badly designed books in spite of their useful contents, or shut my aged, critical eyes to their looks and pay attention only to their contents. Rarely is it possible any longer, in these unfortunate days of mass-produced, technologically ugly books, to have both.

◆

P<small>ROUST'S</small> <small>WAY</small> was right. I found I read, not to expand my narrow geographic horizons or to discover, through a kind of stacking up of sociological detail, the lives other than my own and my friends', but to be enlightened about fictional *method*, about how to use inner resources, memories of experience. Exploration of the private past and what becomes of it during the ameliorating or denigrating light of present memory, Proust's fictional method, was a valuable lesson for a writer.

Any writer? I suppose not. *This* writer, because what is left in old age is the past. I needed to search for the best means of retrieval and use, a printout of memory. I have found no one who has done this better than Proust. I find intimidating the thought that his should be the only method, with all his resultant (and unemulatable) rich, extended similes, comparisons, illustrations, and metaphors, his sumptuous superstructure erected over the germ (in Henry James's term) of minuscule, past event: a cookie, a kiss, a flower. . . .

One evening recently I had an embarrassing failure that showed me how impatient I had become with the present. The Fisherman's Friend, a local eatery much favored by residents, opened (it was early April) after its winter of darkness. Sybil and I and two friends went across the bridge, the daunting causeway, and down Deer Isle to Stonington, to celebrate at the unpretentious place our release from months of eating at home.

For more than an hour, while we ate, feeling grateful that someone else had cooked it and would clean up afterward, the talk flowed freely, without a pause. It was the customary gossip: the fate of some restaurants, the projected date of the opening of others, the illnesses of persons on our peninsula, the deaths of others, the logistic details of trips they had taken and we might take, the present state of employment and health of relatives, and money, money wasted, invested, saved, the cost of things, things and money.

It must have been because I had spent the winter absorbed in Proust and entertained by Don DeLillo, Jim Crace, Penelope Fitzgerald, the new translation of Kafka, Ian McEwan, Nick Hornby, and oddly, Bishop John Spong writing on the Resurrection that I could find nothing to add to the topics that interested the others. I was struck dumb by my inability to contribute anything, or perhaps by impolite boredom with the minutiae of the near-present, the now. I could not find an opening in the flow of talk in which to insinuate a remark about the world of books in which I had been living, so I was silent.

I was asked about the state of my omnipresent shingles. I found I could not say anything about it, so I shrugged, indicating not the absence of pain (for in truth it was constant) but my indifference to discussing it. I was remembering Alain de Botton, in his witty book, *How Proust Can Change Your Life*, quoting the novelist on the subject: "To ask pity for our body is like discoursing in front of an octopus, to which our words can have no more meaning than the sound of the tides."

Of course, had I been a true Proustian, I would have taken in every tittle of gossip and stored it away for later (if it is not too late for me to think of "later") use, to serve as seeds for larger considerations, for some cosmic meditations on significant aspects of human life. One needs to be capable, however, of that kind of extension. In these days I found it harder and harder to do. Minutiae occupied me more than universal observations. In the same way, my handwriting has grown smaller in old age, meaning, I believe, that I have begun to devalue what I have to say, or better, to have become aware of its unimportance. Little matters are best, most honestly and graphically represented by small script.

◆

I CONTINUED TO correspond with friends who are "away" by handwritten letters (once, would not this phrase have been a tautology?). I was aware of the existence of E-mail, voice mail, fax, and other such fast devices, but for me to use such methods would only be bragging, showing off an unexpected prowess in one so old, and not a letter bearing all the marks of the old person writing it.

The act of letter-writing itself has become outdated. I wondered if my devotion to it was self-indulgent, if it was a sign that I was communicating more with myself than with the intended recipient, if I was "describing" events and emotional states to establish their existence for myself, as Virginia Woolf wrote.

Others I know, even a good friend who is by profession a writer, dislike letter-writing and seldom answer my long, perhaps illegible epistles. Another constant communicator and critic of my work (I don't know him personally) who lives in California and uses his computer for his long, literate letters, nervily ended his recent one by requesting that I adopt a more legible form for my replies, like typing or the computer.

I concluded, as I pursued my seemingly isolated pen-to-paper acts that for me, as for many other writers, letter-writing was a means of explication, a sounding board for my impressions, ideas, and observations, rather than a matter of communication. The receivers are not there to interrupt with their (unwanted?) contributions to the discussion. Often, a long silence greeted my discourse, the proper response, I suppose, to one whose conversation tends toward illegible monologue.

◆

My INTEREST in the practice of private prayer fortunately occupied a little of the time I might have spent in worry. I came upon the subject while rereading Graham Greene's *The Heart of the Matter*, when Scobie kneels to say his prayers before going into the confessional—the Our Father, the Hail Mary, rehearsing the Act of Contrition, all so automatic a litany that he is afflicted, Greene writes, by "the awful languor of routine." After he makes his confession and leaves the booth, he feels no relief because the words of absolution "were a formula . . . a hocus pocus."

How does one escape the inevitable reduction to the trite,

the commonplace, the "awful languor of routine" of prayer? I wrote once that I hoped it would happen through the maturing of mind (perhaps with the aid of suffering), during which one finds language of one's own. George Santayana, who speaks openly of "soul," a usage I would avoid, says that "the development of the soul could arise only through an initiation of pain," and then "The soul, too, has her virginity and must bleed a little before bearing fruit." Pain and its resultant suffering, the concomitants of maturity, may provide some way out of deadening custom, some help in formulating original words of prayer.

◆

ONE MORNING in April, at almost five, I sat waiting for the light to come up. Behind me were all the chairs and little tables with which we have equipped the morning room. With my back to them, I thought about how little I am aware of furniture. What is important to me is the window from which I could watch the meadow, the water, the far coast of Deer Isle, the bowl of sky interrupted only (in this morning light) by the black tops of firs and the bare skeleton of the old oak tree.

In my lap was the list of persons I wanted to invite to the July party. I was distracted from it by the slow arrival of light over the cove, a ceremony I was always compelled to watch until it seemed I had left the house and was standing at the water, engrossed in the seductive display of light and color.

Why had the outside eclipsed the interior of the house? It must be that, as the prospects within me darkened, like the inevitability of sunset to a bright day, I looked for sustenance to the intensity and breadth of light outdoors. My chair is built on a swivel so I can turn easily from early-morning concern with the list and the scratchy words on the clipboard to the brilliant path of glory that is the sunrise.

◆

An acquaintance who lives across the Reach on Deer Isle reported a visit to her family at Easter in a distant city. "There was," she said, "a lot of talk but not much conversation."

◆

After much agonizing I decided to buy new clothes, two "outfits," as my granddaughter calls them, for the party. I collected some current catalogs, the mail-order stores in which my shopping is now done. I went through them slowly, turning down the corners of pages on which there were possible choices and then considering, no, *translating* would be a more accurate word, the glamorous photographs of tall, slender, handsome young women on the pages into a realistic self-portrait of me, the elderly, shapeless person that I am. That outfit looks fine on her, I agreed, but on me? No, not likely. . . .

So I put the catalogs aside, thinking that such purchases were beyond me. They would represent a degree of finality, a recognition that, because they were expensive and well made, they would surely outlast their wearer. But still, and more cheerfully, perhaps, such an indulgence would be a sign to those who would come to the party that, beneath the elegantly clothed exterior there dwelled a still-living old person with a vestige of caring about how she looked.

◆

As I prayed one morning, sunk deep into my usual despair at the silence that engulfed me, I found in my notebook Martin Luther's sentence: "God answers our prayers by refusing them."

◆

Now I knew why I admired the work of novelist Nicholson Baker. I had just finished reading his recent *Room Temperature*, taking notice of his fine, parsimonious use of time, language, and space. The timespan of the book is twenty minutes, which occupies 116 pages. In that time he describes his thoughts as he feeds his baby, whom he calls The Bug. In very short space he is able to establish his burning love for the infant and his wife. Baker can write well about almost anything that crosses his mind, without the customary expansion and verbal indulgence that novelists in our time often resort to. In his novels, small is very beautiful, brevity is the soul of fictional conviction and persuasion, intensity is achieved by few words.

◆

FRANK CONROY, who heads the Iowa Writers' Workshop, asked me for a piece he wants to use in a book of thoughts on writing by (who else?) twenty-five writers. It did not take very long to do this, since my opinions on the subject are pretty well set in concrete, like those sayings on monuments to presidents in the Capitol.

In the week before the party, I sent him what I called "A View of Writing Fiction from a Rear Window." Like most aged writers living in the late nineties, I wrote, I had advanced (no, *moved*) from handwriting to the fine, slow loud manual typewriter to the perpetually humming urgings of an electric one, and then, inevitably with the times, to the silent, fast, often helpful but somehow odious computer. I questioned the omnipresence of the current megabook, the logorrhea brought on by the existence of the word processor. I expressed my suspicion that programmed thesauruses would end in uniform language: every user of the machine would have resorted to the same limited supply of synonyms.

Not for the first time, I expanded upon my distrust of the contemporary practice of "promotion" for publications, including the somewhat oxymoronic "book tour," the affection that most writers and all affluent publishers have for public appearances of writers on radio and television, for interviews and readings, *und so weiter.* I rambled on about the substitution (in the public's eye) of the writers' personae for their work. I ended this iconoclastic screed against the present and celebration of the irretrievable past on a surprisingly optimistic note:

> *But still:* in spite of all this elderly invective, I have a curious, unreasonable, almost mystical hope that, in some out-of-the-way place, some cabin in the north woods of Maine, or in a rented room in a large city, there sits a person who is indifferent, even deaf, to the seductions of fame and enriching publishing, who spends endless days and nights, even years, wrestling with the art of the word and the sentence, searching for insights, images, metaphors, felicitous phrasing, original ideas, and hoping for ultimate success, not on Larry King's show or *Oprah,* but for the perfect transfer onto paper of a world that burns in that writer's mind.
>
> I can know nothing of the writer's name or color or sex, or age, for that matter. But it may well be that this is the writer whose singular vision and enduring achievement will be in the hands of twenty-first-century readers.

◆

So MUCH for that explosion. While I was writing the piece for Conroy I was aware of how much my eyesight had improved this summer. After the removal of cataracts, a cloud had lifted from each eye. Print resumed its old, bright self. But I wondered: would this new optical clarity convey to more important matters such as judgment, reasoning? Would my mental faculties benefit from the surgery? It was something to hope for.

◆

I CONTINUED TO come upon interesting arguments against private prayer. I learned from Edward Mendelson's biography (*The Later Auden*) that the poet believed, together with Dom Gregory Dix, that "modern individualistic prayer both impoverishes and falsifies the corporate prayer of the Church. . . ." Participating in devout corporate prayers validates any private praying we may do, thought Dix. We cannot substitute our own solitary prayer for the prayers of the church through its priests.

Why should this be, I wonder. We were single before we were members. We came into life and depart it alone. As children we looked to God for assistance and comfort, even reassurance. Only later, when we subscribed to ritual, did we pray "together." But I believe that God may be as attentive to the solitary voice as to the full-voiced chorus.

◆

IN THE early morning I picked up the *London Review of Books* and read that Robert Musil first thought he wanted to finish his novel, *The Man Without Qualities*, but, Michael Wood the reviewer wrote, "he came to regard all finishing as a wounding of what might have been and can no longer imagine, an end that wouldn't also be a wreck. . . ."

So he, like Marcel Proust and other early-twentieth-century novelists, "fell in love with the interminable work, the book that seemed interminable." There would be no need for an ending, no limitation on the endless possibilities of the fiction.

This is the way we experience life. For most lives we encounter we never learn the ending; events happen without their conclusion. But most fiction is satisfactorily rounded off. It is tempting to end the final sentence of a novel without a period, so that the reader will come away from the book with the feeling that the story goes on . . .

♦

FROM THE Boston Book Fair Sybil brought home two cookbooks, one written in 1911. I scanned them both, because I was in the process of considering what to serve at the party. I stopped at interesting recipes to consider their applicability to my enterprise.

Then I discovered an odd thing, that I was fonder of reading about food than eating it. An elegant, complicated recipe gave me pleasure. There is something pure about food on the page that is, for some reason, adulterated in the process of consumption. The acts of choosing, preparing, serving, cutting, forking, lifting it without accident to the mouth, and then the concern that it will be digested properly, and then of course the inelegant end result, the elimination of it without too much effort: the whole process has very little grace. Repeating it three times a day seems to lower the human person in my regard. Animals, often called, wrongly, beasts, do not read before they eat, so their meals have the virtue of a kind of natural cleanliness.

♦

YESTERDAY THERE arrived in the mail a book of Berenice Abbott's photographs published by the New York Public Library from its collection. I spent much of the morning living in those fine pictures, walking fast under the great clock on Fifth Avenue and Forty-fourth Street, sitting on top of the #19 bus from Riverside Drive, riding across Fifty-seventh Street and down Fifth Avenue to Washington Square, looking up at the intricate iron structure that upheld the Third Avenue El, passing the brownstone bathed in curious light at the end of Fifth Avenue on my way to college at the Square (very much like the painting of a row of houses by Edward Hopper), considering the wall of wonderful, cheap choices of food at the Automat on Eighth Avenue, reading the covers of magazines at the corner newsstand at Thirty-second Street and Third Avenue.

Abbott's was my city, my time when I was young, in the last five years of the thirties, my heated waiting room from the wind of the El, my admired Chrysler Building, my docks and bridges, shuttered warehouses, tenements, excavations. Most unsettling to me, the old native of the city, was her photograph of the Blossom Restaurant at 103 Bowery, a block down from my father's men's furnishing store at 88 Bowery, gone now for more than fifty years. I remember that restaurant. My mother and I walked past it on the way to the store. Next door to it was a seven-foot barber's pole, the top half of which had constantly rotating stripes. The sign over the door said that a shave, with bay rum and hot towel, cost ten cents. On the window of the restaurant the price of offerings was written in chalk: a vegetable dinner was ten cents, roast leg of veal, twenty, and the most expensive dish listed, "two large pork chops," would cost thirty cents.

For the entire day I was sunk in nostalgia, as if the black-and-white past in Abbott's photographs and my memory of those places had come alive together and obliterated the green lawn and meadow, and the blue cove of the present. The scrim of worn city structures and Elevateds, the concrete landscape, architecture, and streets of my young life, had effected a resurrection of the past.

◆

WE BEGAN to fix our old house for the time when guests would be here for the party. The sagging Victorian sofa needed to be fitted with a new, sturdy leg. The grandfather clock required a house call from Mr. Deuchech, a courtly clock expert who comes with costly regularity to fix the old timepiece. The claw-footed bathtub upstairs, stained yellow with use and age, had to be sprayed with an odorous plastic material to renew its surface. The garden circle had to be redone so that we could back out of the new garage without displacing stones every day. As usual, the trim on the sea-facing side of the house required repainting.

These repairs meant there would be people in and about, that my cherished solitude would be disturbed. It was foolish, but such activity, necessary as it is, seemed to add to my level of stress and thus to the lingering pain of post-herpetic neuralgia, an affliction that remains after shingles.

But there was another occasion for foolish worry. For some time Sybil had envisioned a stone patio to fill the triangular space created by the recent construction of a garage and the small connecting room between the porch and the garage. So she decided this might be a good time to put it down. She foresaw a pleasant area where our guests could have their drinks on their way to the tent we planned to erect on the lawn.

We found a chap who did such work and contracted with

him. This caused me to begin my inevitable days of worry: would he arrive on time, finish on time? Would the displaced grass grow back? Truckloads of sand, then gravel, then paving bricks arrived erratically, rutting the side and back grass and dumping huge loads of material on other sections of lawn.

There was no end of old things to be repaired and new ones to be constructed, about all of which I would need to worry.

Everyone who has lived in an old house, and happens to be old themselves, has seen the resemblance between it and an aging body. Something is always going wrong in them both. One piece of the structure wears out just after a repair has been made elsewhere. A new part becomes essential. The fine wholeness of a new house and a young body gives way in time, inevitably, to similar ailments: rickety structure, leaking orifices, sagging parts, and worn, ineffective equipment.

◆

AND WERE these mountainous, ridiculous concerns not enough, I found I worried about the new kitten. The concern was much like what I had, more than fifty years ago, about my first baby: Is she eating enough? Too much? Is she cold in the odd places she chooses to sleep? Is she lonely when we go out to dinner? *Is she happy?*

Absurd.

◆

TWENTY DAYS remained until the event. I was suffering from cold feet. I thought endlessly about the concept of "party." Celebration. Why did I feel we must celebrate together? Why was I not willing to hold a solitary party to celebrate my having achieved, at long last, some small, peaceful connection with my inner self. I thought I might hold a rehearsal for the final state, nonbeing, the time after the distinguished thing, as Henry James termed it, has arrived, the unique period when I will be forever alone. In this sense, social gatherings are deceptive: they effectively disguise the true nature of the end of our lives. They cover it with people and talk so that we are distracted from the inevitable future.

Early one July morning, when I could not sleep and while I was engaged in all this dour thought, I thought of Mrs. Dalloway's party day. I came downstairs to locate the book and re-read Virginia Woolf's masterpiece. I read until I finished the book, and then went out on the porch to savor the wan, early sunshine, the small sailboats moving around their anchors in the cove, the empty, bright blue sky. The air had only a hint of salt.

When I went back in to *Mrs. Dalloway* I found Woolf's exact simile for my day: ". . . what a morning—fresh as if issued to children on a beach," she writes as Clarissa Dalloway comes out of her London house on a June morning soon after the end of World War I. She is going to shop for last-minute things for the evening's event: "All was for the party."

Her old lover Peter, returned from a long absence abroad and invited to her party at the last minute, asks her: "What's the sense of your parties?"

Clarissa answers that she gives parties as "an offering, to combine disparate persons," someone from one section of London, someone else from another. Her party was to be ". . . an offering for the sake of offering . . . it was her gift."

So. This was the way to think about it, to enjoy bringing together persons from every era of my life, children and grandchildren, Sybil's sister and brothers who had never met the members of my family, even after we had lived together for twenty-five years, people here and people from away, writers who were my literary friends and people from the publishing house with which I was associated, my literary agent and his novelist wife, new friends and very old ones, neighbors here and friends from Washington, D.C.

The party then, like Mrs. Dalloway's, would be a gathering of disparate persons, an offering (but what is it I have to offer beside food and drink?), a gift to myself. Then I thought: the gift I have to offer to those who came from a distance is this small spot in Maine, this view of a quiet sea, this peace and se-clusion. Because I have always selfishly held the place close to myself, with only Sybil to share it, I will let go of it for a few days. I will be hospitable to the presence of others. All was for the party.

◆

I HAVE DECIDED that Paul Valéry's dictum "A poem is never finished; it is abandoned" is true, in part, of life as well. But it is life that abandons us. We may well have the feeling that it is un-finished. We do not often, voluntarily, leave it.

◆

LIZ BROWN, a former student, sent me the sentences she read on a board in front of a Maine church: "Be an organ donor. Give your heart to Jesus."

◆

I LEFT OFF watching the sky darken over the cove and went with Sybil to see the movie that had been touted as the best of the year, *Saving Private Ryan*. It was brilliant, and hard to watch. Sometimes I think that the high points of my life were the years of that war, which seemed to most of us at the time to have been a justified one, unlike the others that followed. We were awash in warm patriotism, very young yet willing for the first time in our young lives to follow orders, content to live with ration stamps and blackout. We ate and drank ourselves merry, for tomorrow. . . . And yet, watching the first half hour of the movie, seeing an infantryman land on Omaha Beach under terrible gunfire and then retrieve his shot-off arm from the bloody water and carry it ashore, I realized how little I knew of the horror of even that "justified" war.

I once thought that those were happy years, and so they were, for us living safely on this continent with our small inconveniences. But for the thousands who died, or were grievously wounded (like my former husband who was shot on Okinawa), or drowned in the wash of Omaha Beach, the hell of war ended in death. For them, there was no justification for the war.

◆

THE KITTEN has taken up self-satisfied residence in our house. She has seven places to sleep, she eats when she feels like it, she uses as playthings any object she finds, precious or not. We say no to many of her more destructive activities but, as my daughter reminded me, to a cat, no is not a command, it is an opinion. "That's what you think" is the way Kitty Kelley deals with a command. "I don't happen to agree."

I have decided that I like her because she is everything that I am not, a reminder of what I once was. She is agile and young, she has undiminished energy and curiosity, she has a long life ahead of her. She represents my early youth, when all those things were mine.

I like her. I envy her.

◆

JACK SHOEMAKER, an acquaintance from the days when he headed North Point Press in California, a company that made a practice of housing good texts in beautiful books, sent me Peter Brooks's autobiography, *Thread of Time*. I had never seen any of Brooks's theatrical productions, but his descriptions of his original uses of bare stages, few costumes, and unfettered improvisation to communicate meaning to an audience persuaded me that this was a fruitful way for live theater to go. I had seen many plays that were so elaborately staged and costumed, disguising the simple uses of the human body, that the significance of the play itself was lost.

Once again it was heartening to come upon another example of the beauty and significance of less.

◆

CONTINUING, CONSTANT worries: Will it rain on the day I am planning the outdoor lobster dinner? Will a tent be sufficient? Will it be possible to serve the lobsters hot? The wine and champagne cold? Will the caterer, a friend, Bob MacDonald (I hadn't heard from him in weeks), bring off all the elaborate arrangements? Will Duke remember to come two days before to mow the lawn before the tent goes up? Will it arrive on time? And what will we do with the kitten during all the confusion of the party? Will she get out? The number of worries piled up and I began to wonder why I ever conceived of the idea of a weekend celebration for this birthday. Why celebrate being eighty? Why not mourn, have a wake?

When Sybil and I were making reservations at a nearby inn and motel for the people from away, and deciding on the offerings and the seating for the first dinner at a local restaurant, my mountain of concern grew higher. Would all these unconnected persons, literary and local, young and old, one family and another unknown to them, get along, mix well, "socialize," as they say?

For some reason I was comforted in this mental turmoil by the thought of the ghosts of the nonguests who would be eerily present under the tent. Richard Lucas, priest-friend from early teaching days, was the first person I knew in the backward city of Albany to march, in his black suit and collar, in a parade of gay persons, for what cause I cannot now remember.

Everyone thought it was a brave, sacerdotal act and no one, except his close priest friends on the faculty, knew he was gay. One vindictive priest, jealous perhaps, accused him of homosexuality to the college president, a man who had come to his job fresh from heading the Air Force Academy and had brought with him a militant, unilateral approach to governance of a college. At once, he notified the two accused priests they would not be reappointed.

The near-riot that this decision caused was extraordinary for a Catholic girls' college in that time, the sixties. Nuns and students, lay faculty members and staff, joined in signing a petition. The students staged a sit-down, demanding that the trustees fire the president. After much resistance, they did. The removal of the two priests was rescinded. Peace once again reigned over the quiet, sedate campus.

But the tragedy, in one sense, was to come. Father Lucas told his friends he could be closeted no longer. Shocked by the scandal in which he was a principal, he left the campus, the priesthood, the church. He could run but he could not hide, as Joe Louis said. He went to New York City and at once found a job at Doubleday. I didn't see him again in the years during which he rose in the hierarchy of publishing in San Francisco.

What his personal life was like in that open city I can only conjecture. With the restraints of his collar gone, I think Richard may have ardently entered into the life of bars, baths, and one-night unions where the realization of his true self was possible. He formed a permanent union with a handsome Mayan man and lived and prospered in a small town in Marin County. What more I know is that when we met again at a university press meeting at Harvard his charming youthfulness had been transformed: he was gray and feeble and thin. He was dying of AIDS.

We sat together on steps near the Fogg Museum in wan Cambridge sunshine and talked of our lives, mine containing a same-sex choice similar to his but without his difficulties and traumas, and without the terrible price he was paying for his freedom.

I saw him again in Oneonta, where his parents lived and where he had gone to say good-bye to them. He was having trouble walking, even with his handsome, British ash cane, and he needed help getting into my car. We lunched together in a nearby tearoom, and once again we rehearsed our lives since the college debacle. I remember that he assured me he did not regret his decision to make a new life for himself, although it had hurt his parents and he was sorry for that. He would have been safe if he had stayed within the strictures of the church, he acknowledged, but he had some good, satisfying, *free* years, and he had no regrets. He said he only regretted that he was now too sick to travel to England to occupy his customary seats in Wimbledon, but he had bought tickets for the Metropolitan Opera's new productions of the *Ring* in April, and he was planning to go.

It did not happen. He died in California. Months later we

celebrated his life in a New York apartment with his friends from publishing and the church and the college. Now somewhat unsteady on my feet, I used the ash cane he sent me, a replica of his. In some way, in some form, I believe, he made it to Wimbledon and to the *Ring*, and in some shape he may be at the party.

◆

Oᴏꜰᴛᴇɴ, ꜰᴜʟʟ of anxiety about the party, I went over to our bookstore across the path from the house to comfort myself with the sight of books being inspected by the kind of interested customers Wayward Books attracts in late spring and early summer.

Anatole Broyard, who ended his career as a regular book reviewer for the *New York Times*, once had a bookstore in Greenwich Village. It was a natural transition from his boyhood when "books were our weather, our environment, our clothing. We didn't simply read books; we became them." He began by stocking his favorite books—Kafka, Wallace Stevens, D. H. Lawrence, Céline. He discovered that those eminent books did not fill the shelves of his shop, so he went to Fourth Avenue, where there used to be rows of good but grubby bookstores, and fleshed out his stock.

Broyard advertised in literary quarterlies that he wished to buy books, but this announcement had little effect on collectors in the Village "who had more books than money." Furthermore they all had severe cases of "separation anxiety," so some depressed sellers undervalued their books, and some more avid ones ("hysterical" is Broyard's word for them) asked high prices for them because "it was their souls they were selling." As he said, "Pricing an out-of-print book is one of the most poignant forms of criticism."

He was advised by a customer that his shop was too neat, too "cheerful." "A bookshop should have an almost ecclesiastical atmosphere . . . an odor, or redolence, of snuffed candles, dryness, desuetude—even contrition." Broyard's customers were people who had nothing else to do, who were friendless, without pleasures or resources. They wanted to tell him about their lives, bringing back into the store "all the clutter, the cast-off odds and ends of their lives."

Clearly this combination of inadequacies—plus financial exigencies, I would imagine—drove him out of the book trade. Sybil, the active partner (I have always been the very silent partner) in Wayward Books for twenty-five years, the store that moved from a basement to two locations on Capitol Hill, and finally came to rest in a building Sybil had built in Sargentville, shared some of Broyard's experiences. Early she observed that book buyers like a certain amount of untidiness, stacks of books on the floor, on tables, a general air of disorder despite the care she takes to organize. She, like Broyard, has occasional visitors who are clearly bored by books. They are waiting out a ride to a restaurant. They want to use the outhouse, or they are aliterate spouses waiting impatiently for the book-loving other. Or, it is a rainy day and they can think of nothing else to do.

Her customers sometimes tell her the story of their lives, some of which she finds interesting and then she summarizes the narrative for me when she comes home. Sometimes the stories are heartbreaking. She weeps as she relates them. As Broyard wrote: "In the contest between life and literature, life wins every time."

◆

I WAS ASTONISHED to read in the glossy *Times* Sunday magazine section last week the effect that famed editor Gordon Lish had on the early work of even more famous minimalist writer Raymond Carver. At the Lilly Archives a literary researcher named D. T. Max studied manuscripts of Carver stories. He found they were covered with large slash marks almost cutting some stories in half, and inserts that changed the order of sentences, paragraphs, etc. Whole sentences and paragraphs were excised, or sentences transferred to other places in the story.

The effect of such severe editing was to sharpen, even change, the force of the stories. Since Raymond Carver's reputation rested on these stories (he was regarded as the first minimalist)—his poetry is not distinguished—it appeared that Lish was almost a collaborator in his work, even, in some cases, its dominant partner.

What could one make of all this? Gordon Lish is known as a difficult man, highly opinionated about fiction, and usually treating with scorn any prose style except his own pared-down, less-is-far-better preference. After leaving Knopf, he held classes at Columbia University, ousting decorative writers by his derisive comments about their work. Some left, embarrassed and furious.

At the Iowa workshop I had a student whose first (and only, thus far) novel was edited by Lish. The prose of Rudy Wilson's *The Red Truck* bears a close resemblance to Carver's. Wilson's novel begins:

Ned was dead a year; his bed was cold and silent. Mama K died after he did. She was my grandmother. Her face always reminded me of corn. She lived in a pink room. My parents were far away in the new room, in the back of the house.

We were all there, by ourselves, with everybody else in the world.

We lived on a hill above the dirt road that led to the orphanage. They had the steel push merry-go-round. I thought of it, so still and shiny in the night. The wind blew on it.

Enough. Enough to see the slashing hand of Gordon Lish through these sentences. Rudy Wilson wrote to the *Times* after the appearance of Max's article: "He took my novel to France for a month and mowed it down from 440 pages to a final 178. He said to me when it was done, 'I wish I could put my name on it.' I thought, You may as well." After his shock at this brutal cutting (Lish had also taken a line out of context and used it as the final sentence of the book) he agreed that Lish had done his main job, which was to cut in order to get at the meat of the work, a task at which he is a genius, concluded Rudy Wilson.

I see the efficacy of this for books that begin by being badly overwritten. But I shudder to think what Lish would have done to *Remembrance of Things Past* or *War and Peace* or *Moby-Dick* or *The Ambassadors* had these masterpieces fallen under his hand in the years he was an editor at Knopf. It would have been easy to get at the meat of Melville's work, for example, by cutting out all the cetology. And I can see Lish making the narrator an unnamed figure throughout the book so he could conclude the manuscript with the stark sentence "Call me Ishmael."

Raymond Carver never acknowledged Lish's strong role in his work. But he placed all his manuscripts in a library where they would be available to the public. It was as if he were willing for the truth to be known after his death, a posthumous tribute to the editor who was responsible for his achievement.

◆

I USED TO joke about the Collyer brothers, whose sad life was finally revealed in their obituary. They died in their Fifth Avenue house, with their old car, which they kept in a room in the house, and their extraordinary accumulation of newspapers stacked almost to the ceiling. The piles collapsed, blocking the doors and preventing the elderly brothers from escaping.

But recently I stopped making fun of the saving habits of the Collyers. I learned that the able-to-see brother, who was feeding his sibling health foods, herbs, and vegetables in the belief that they would restore his health, was saving the stacks of *New York Times* so that his brother could read them when, cured by his diet, he regained his sight.

◆

A LETTER CAME from a right-wing Catholic church group asking me to send money to support its pro-life efforts. It brought to mind Daniel Maguire's recently published letter in the *Times*. A professor of moral theology at Marquette University, he cites two historical examples of the early Christian Church's defense of the practice of abortion to save a woman's life. Saint Antoninus, archbishop of Florence, a fifteenth-century Dominican, was responsible for the first treatise on the subject. He wrote that an early abortion to save the life of a woman was moral. And Thomas Sanchez, a seventeenth-century Jesuit, said that all of his contemporaneous Catholic theologians justified abortion under the same conditions.

The church's harsh anti-abortion position, Maguire points out, is entirely a phenomenon of the twentieth century. . . . So much for our belief in our present enlightened state. I have come to believe that often so-called progress works in reverse, to the rear, as the marching command has it. We are moving ahead in time, but walking steadily backward in many other ways.

◆

EVERY MORNING I had been using Thomas Merton's prayer from *Thoughts in Solitude* to start my hour of meditation. It begins: "My Lord God, I have no idea where I am going. I do not see the road ahead of me. I cannot know for certain where it will end. Nor do I really know myself, and the fact that I think I am following your will does not mean that I am actually doing so. . . ."

I liked this prayer, I trusted it, because it is full of my own doubts and uncertainty. The force of its negatives is better than the bland assurances, the mindless certainties of most prayers. As for Merton, for me the future always seems full of fog and peril, and the promises of resurrection somewhat difficult to accept. Preachers always seem to be so sure of what God wants of us, what His will is, whereas I am uncertain about those matters because I do not know the source of their authority. How do they know, how do I, or Merton, know, what God wants?

◆

AN EARLY copy of *The Presence of Absence* arrives, my book about private prayer that I planned to give to guests at the party. In the same mail came a volume I had sent for, the Quaker Elizabeth Gray Vining's book, *The World in Tune*. In it I found the ending to one of Cardinal Fénelon's fine (and useful) prayers. "Teach me to pray. Pray thyself in me." There was another useful piece of advice which I took to heart while I prayed that day. His faithful follower and later collaborator,

Madame Guyon, wrote to Fénelon when he was appointed tutor to the Duke of Burgundy: "Act always regardless to self. The less you have of self, the more you will have of God."

Vining gave me another good paragraph, from George Mac-Donald: " 'O God,' I said, and that was all. But what are the prayers of the whole universe more than the expansion of that one cry? It is not what God can give us, but God that one wants."

◆

At long last Bob MacDonald came to call, he who will orchestrate and cater the whole affair. He took copious notes about what to order, about the tent, about the timing of everything: the lobsters will be delivered hot at exactly seven o'clock, the tent will be set up the day before to ensure that it will fit the narrow space, the wine and the case of champagne, a gift of my gala-arranging daughter in New York, will be properly iced and uncorked when needed.

I could think of nothing else to tell him that I was worried about at the moment, but this did not guarantee that, at three o'clock in the morning, I would not think of other things. Giving a party for sixty dissimilar friends, the first such occasion in my eighty years of life, I found myself joining George Mac-Donald in his cry: "O God."

◆

The next day the Swarthmore College *Bulletin* arrived. It is a sixty-five-page glossy publication sent to Sybil, class of '52, my friend and companion of twenty-five years. But I read every issue faithfully and was always intrigued by the level of achievement, prosperity, happiness, entire contentment with their lives, and national, even world recognition that the alumni reported. They all seemed to be proud parents and grandparents of Swarthmore offspring who, in turn, became professors, writers, research scientists, vice presidents for operations of large corporations, Ph.D.s, and MBAs.

The older ones were constant travelers. They encountered members of their class in such places as Germany, Crete, Greece, Kyoto, Japan, Australia, or they clustered happily in one or another of the Kendall senior retirement residences (founded by the Quakers), where they seemed to be as active, tireless, and productive as ever.

All the early achievers (and they seemed all to be *high* achievers) continued to achieve: "Dick Moses, '40, after a career in publishing, celebrated his 81st birthday by receiving a Ph.D. in English from Temple University." Frank Fairman, '45, said that his music was being performed in Olomouc, the Czech republic. Of course the earlier classes reported the deaths of their members, but still, the dominant note in those reports is of happy lives, even in retirement communities: "Jack ('41) is chair of the fitness committee, a member of the religious affairs and endowment fund committees . . . writes for the White Horse newspaper, is a member of the chorus, leads the singing every week at our before-dinner wine-and-cheese party."

The enduring iconoclast in me wondered if the *Bulletin* ever received an account of a different sort of life. Of course I realized it was only successes who submitted the happy details of their lives to alumnae journals. I was tempted to write a contrary entry:

"After three failed marriages and the death of my only son by suicide following his expulsion from Harvard for drug-dealing, I found myself with almost no funds and debts amounting to five figures, mostly his college loans. I declared bankruptcy and retired to a used mobile home in the Maine woods where I am engaged (seasonally) in blueberry picking, wreath-making, and kitchen work at a girls camp. I have not encountered any classmates in the forty years since graduation, and my economic situation has made it impossible for me to come to reunions. I am not, to be honest, looking forward to very much. A clinic doctor says I should have my badly arthritic knees replaced, but I have put that off because of lack of health insurance. I am collecting a very small social security check which pays for food, together with food stamps, and grocery bags from the weekly Island Pantry handout. I regret not being able to contribute to the Alumni Collection, but I wish you success in the drive."

◆

IN THE years before the party I was slowly shedding my old habit of speed reading. It once served me well when I was reviewing books, sometimes two or three a week. But now I discovered that I was compelled to read fast only when the book, a mystery usually, was all plot. Suspense made me race ahead, ignoring what seemed to be unnecessary detail or red herrings. But the books I was now reading—Barbara Kingsolver's *The Poisonwood Bible* and Ian McEwan's *Amsterdam* and all the works of David Storey and Jim Crace I could find, rereading Marilynne Robinson's remarkable first novel, *Housekeeping*, and the new translation of Franz Kafka's *The Castle*—all serious works of character or theme, I read slowly, savoring the good prose and the artful development of the story.

I resolved in the future to read only such books as would demand that I abandon my lifelong bad habit of hasty reading. Slow is beautiful would be my directive.

◆

WHEN GIL Harrison, revered friend from the time I worked for him, heard of my age about to be celebrated, he wrote to me: "O, to be eighty again." So relative are the stages of old age.

◆

IN LATE February we visited places in which to put up our visitors from away. Panic had overtaken me when I heard there were to be two weddings that same July weekend. I realized how few inns and B and Bs there were near us; our peninsula was not especially hospitable to tourists. I liked this about it, of course, except when I am the host to thirty-two guests from away. We went to two places, inspected them, found them satisfactory, and made reservations for those who were coming from a distance. One worry had been laid to rest.

When we got home, having successfully managed the hazards of ice on the roads and snow coming down to disguise it, Kitty Kelley came to the door and made a great show of having missed us: one cannot really tell with cats. Such enthusiasm may only be a sign of anticipation of food.

I have learned what it is I like best about this cat: she is utterly silent. When I talk to her (foolishly, it would seem) she cocks her head, raises her ears, and makes no reply. She never meows, as most cats are said to do. Her only sounds are little, almost inaudible grunts when she is hungry or emotionally disturbed in any way. There is something reassuring about her habitual silence. It is as if nothing in this world is worth responding to. I think this is the same omnipresent silence that Ezra Pound maintained at the end of his life, a judicious, judgmental, but mute response to the chattering world. I find it pleasant.

◆

A LETTER CAME yesterday asking me to contribute to a book to be composed of "famous Maine writers." I thought the adjective gratuitous, intended to flatter the recipient. In my case it did not succeed because I am well aware that I am not a famous writer, only one that is known a little among a small audience of readers.

But more mistaken was the designation "Maine" writer. Because I had lived in the state for a little more than ten years, I hardly qualified for this designation. For one thing, I had never written about the state except one tiny corner of it, the cove and my house, and small events like trips to the post office and the store, a sixth of a mile away. The secluded three acres and the ever-changing moods and seasons of the cove had provided me with the necessary climate for interior travel. So I had learned very little at firsthand about Maine, only a few things about myself as I lived contentedly here under the favorable conditions that fostered memory and self-exploration.

How presumptuous it would be for me, in my ignorance about native persons, about the conflicts between them and the well-to-do Johnnies-come-lately, the fishing and blueberry-picking and wreath-making culture, to be called a Maine writer. I had brought my subject matter with me from a life lived for almost seventy years in other places. My research here had been entirely inward.

◆

OBSERVING WITH gratitude my silent cat and the subject of salutary silence in general made me think about Beckett. Early in the summer we went to Haystack, a colony of artisans and craftsmen on Deer Isle, not far from us, to hear a friend, Alan Nevelthau, perform two monologues called *Nothing*. Al is a quite-young, handsome actor whose professional devotion is to the plays of Beckett. Dressed in an old overcoat, the usual costume for a Beckett role, he was, in a moment, by means of voice and gesture, transformed into an old man who cries out against the nothingness of his old age.

The audience for this moving display of despair and rebellion against the emptiness of the past, the present, and the approaching Void was, on the whole, young students who enjoyed the old man's sometimes comic and picturesque descriptions of his life. They laughed, they found his pathetic stories and his cries of irrational despair funny. But the few elderly couples present (we among them) were silent and showed no signs of seeing humor in his unbearable accuracy about old age.

So I went home, depressed by Al and Beckett. Next morning I began to reread Ronald Hayman's study of Beckett's plays. Beckett wrote a book on Proust in which he explored the principles Proust (and then Beckett) followed in writing fiction:

> The only fertile research is excavatory, immersive, a contraction of the spirit, a descent. The artist is active, but negatively, shrinking from the nullity of the extracumferential phenomena, drawn into the core of the eddy.

How close to my thinking this came. I empathized with Beckett's spiritually decrepit heroes, with the voiceless and "homeless men and women at the end of their tether, past pose or pretense, past claim of meaningful existence," as Richard Ellmann characterized the people who inhabited Beckett's plays and novels. He was the prophet, the poet of the old. He created few young characters; his oeuvre was populated by the elderly, the no-sayers-in-thunder, and those who spend the end of their lives in misery and despair.

◆

An acquaintance, Althea Van Dusen, told me that her mother accurately described medical care of old age as "the outlay for the upkeep of the downhill."

◆

For almost twenty years I have had Malcolm Cowley's small memoir, *The View from Eighty*, on my shelf without ever reading it. In view of the approaching event, I decided to see how he regarded his eighth decade. It turned out to be a jaunty, lighthearted record of his own old age together with accounts of others, like Florida Scott-Maxwell, Cicero, John Cowper Powys, Ramon Guthrie, all of whom had good later years, all of them creative people who survived into their eighties and nineties still working at their craft.

Cowley turned out to be a mine of interesting stories. From him I learned more about the Collyer brothers, whom he uses as an example of the characteristic untidiness of old age. Cowley enlarged upon the scant details of the 1947 obituary. Langley Collyer had been a concert pianist, Homer an admiralty lawyer. Their section of upper Fifth Avenue had become lower Harlem, so they hid away in their mansion in fear, one surmises, of the neighborhood. Langley played piano for his half-paralyzed, blind brother, and for years saved every daily paper so that, as I have noted, Homer might catch up on them when he regained his sight. This was to be accomplished through his diet of buns and oranges.

The newspapers were stacked and bundled. The bundles reached to the high ceilings and covered every wall. When the police broke down the front door, after a call from an anonymous person, they found the front hall blocked. The narrow passages formed by the stacked newspapers were arranged so that intruders would be trapped by them.

With the aid of a ladder, the police entered through an upstairs window and found Homer in his bathrobe, having starved to death. Eighteen days later, after clearing out piles of other junk that had accumulated, including dismantled parts of a model T Ford (for fifty years I had had a mistaken vision of the complete vehicle hanging from the ceiling of a room, rather like the whole horse in Truman Capote's *Other Voices, Other Rooms*), the police found Langley.

He must have been on his way to Homer's room to bring him food when he was caught in one of his own booby traps, Cowley reported. I pictured two of the stacks of paper falling simultaneously on him. His body had been almost consumed by rats. Carted away by the Department of Sanitation, Malcolm Cowley writes, were 120 tons of rubbish, including the newspapers blind Homer was never to read, fourteen grand pianos that (I like to think) Langley played on to the end, and the parts of the old car.

Everyone laughs at what is called the Langley Collyer syndrome, but I began to have contrary thoughts about the logic of his seemingly obsessive savings. There was his hope for a cure that required saving reading matter in case it happened, the collection of many musical instruments so he could play in any room he found himself. Perhaps he hoped that someday he would want to drive again and so he would have the parts of the car handy to be assembled.

I understood all this in an odd way because my tidy habits run counter to Langley's. After his example I am afraid of accumulation. I throw out everything I believe I do not, and will not need, and often later discover I do. This is so, at the end of my life, my heirs (unlike the Collyer brothers, who had none, I have many) will not find a formidable collection of unused or little-used stuff that they do not want but must deal with.

I thought of my grandmother, who, at the age of ninety-three, would not permit her housekeeper, aged seventy-two, to buy more than two lemons when she went shopping, although she had been assured that buying them by the bag was much cheaper and easier on the number of trips to Broadway the housekeeper had to make. Grandmother feared there would be pieces of lemon left in the icebox after she was gone. As it happened, the housekeeper, the nurse, and I had tea in the late afternoon of her death. We divided the last half of the last lemon into three small slices, thus carrying out her wishes to the final citric drop.

Samuel Beckett used the word *sans* seven times in one of his last French prose pieces, and when he translated it into English, he used "lessness" for what we might have expected to be "without." I prefer "lessness" as both instruction and slogan for my old age.

◆

In *The View from Eighty* I learned that Gil Harrison's sigh about his advanced age originated with Supreme Court Justice Holmes, who lived to be ninety-four. Somewhere about that age, he saw a pretty girl and said (and I quote it again): "O, to be eighty again!"

◆

Again from Cowley: the Catholic poet Paul Claudel wrote in his journal: "No eyes left, no ears, no teeth, no legs, no wind. And when all is said and done, how astonishingly well one does without them." This is the sort of cheeriness I need to tap into, being by nature and preference entirely dyspeptic about the state of bodily decay in old age. I try, hard as I can, to adhere to Cato's axiom: "Old age must be resisted and its deficiencies supplied by taking pains; we must fight old age as we would a disease."

I was slowly learning that only humor and perhaps irony are weapons against the indignities of aging. Cowley was a friend of Bruce Barton, once the editor of *The New Republic*. He reported Barton as having said, "I stagger when I walk, and small children follow me making bets on which way I will go next. This upsets me; children shouldn't gamble."

Cowley reminded me of how often old people resort to the enlivening philosophy of Florida Scott-Maxwell, whose record of her eighty-third year, *The Measure of My Days*, is a classic of gerontic literature. She saw old age as an achievement of sorts. "We who are old know that age is more than a disability. It is an intense and varied experience, almost beyond our capacity at times, but something to be carried high. If it is a long defeat it is also a victory, meaningful for the initiates of time, if not for those who have come less far."

I suppose I have always thought of old age as a long defeat, full of unsuccessful skirmishes with small losses of memory and physical capacity and finally, a lost battle. It is also replete with ironies that sting when they are humorously expressed. Malcolm Cowley tells of an octogenarian "with all his buttons" who said at a testimonial dinner for his senior partner: "They tell you that you'll lose your mind when you grow older. What they don't tell you is that you won't miss it very much." Funny. Terrible.

Scott-Maxwell's victory was a private one. "It has taken me all the time I've had to become myself." And then she added, "If at the end of your life you have only yourself, it is much. Look, you will find."

This reminded me of what Frederick Buechner's elderly mother (reported in his autobiography, *Telling Secrets*) said: "If I didn't have something to look for, I would be lost." The hardest thing to find, after lifelong search, is the self. When Mrs. Buechner, and I with her, succeed in that, there will be, Scott-Maxwell assured us, a real, private celebration. . . . Look . . . and you may find.

Montaigne: "The greatest thing in the world is to know how to belong to myself."

◆

HAVING ABANDONED catalogs, we started off for Bangor to see if we could find clothes for the approaching weekend (our present wardrobes being entirely from the discount store of L. L. Bean in Ellsworth and thus unsuitable for any occasion other than hunting in the woods, digging for clams, or living a hardy, jeans-clad life in a very cold climate).

On the way I saw a number of signs for REDEMPTION. At first sight, once, I had thought this signified a place of worship where an opportunity for atonement and ultimate forgiveness might be offered. It was disappointing to learn it was a store where cans and bottles were returned. . . . On the trip for clothes this time I saw a new sign: INSTANT REDEMPTION. O, that it meant my old misconception, intensified by happening on the spot.

We found nothing suitable or, I should add with the double meaning of the word, fitting, in the many stores at the Bangor Mall. Having driven almost 110 miles in this vain search, I went home, sat in my swivel chair looking out at the green meadow and the high-grass lawn (renewed occasion for concern: will Duke come to mow, in time for the tent to be raised and the patio to be usable?). I rescued some catalogs from the basket and returned to doing my shopping from them.

Instant redemption, in a way.

◆

To TAKE my mind off my worries, I went back to working on a novel, which had been half written when I abandoned it, twice or three times, to write four memoirs. Sybil referred to it as "the stable mate." For me rewriting is a process of reduction, an adoption of the "lessness" of the material. In *The Periodic Table* Primo Levi describes it well, although he was writing about a chemical process in which he was engaged:

> Distillation is beautiful. First of all, because it is a slow, philosophic, and silent occupation . . . it involves a metamorphosis from liquid to vapor (invisible), and from this once again to liquid; but in this double journey, up and down, purity is attained, an ambiguous and fascinating condition . . . from imperfect material you obtain the essence, the *usia*, the spirit. . . .

I thought of the reduction Willa Cather must have exercised when she was writing *A Lost Lady* and *My Mortal Enemy*, surely among the best of her works, condensed, short, and so wholly effective. I remembered Jeannette Haien's fine novella, *The All of It*, her first and most perfect book, May Sarton's very short *As We Are Now*, of all her many novels (to my mind) the best, and James Crace's *The Gift of Stones*. All of these illustrate "the force of few words" (is this Alexander Pope? I think so). I have decided to see *The Habit* in these terms, a mass of material from which I must try to extract the essence.

◆

THE OLDEST thing in our house is a tiny engraving, one-and-a-half by two-and-a-half inches. It is by Albrecht Altdorfer, who lived between 1480 and 1538, and was called "most sympathetic of all the Little Masters to us in our age, the eldest and most independent." He lived in Regensberg, Germany, and was called the lesser Albrecht in contrast to Dürer. But the scholar H. W. Singer claims that "no other artist, not even Dürer, puts as deep feeling into his work as does he."

My engraving was a gift sent to me by a former student. It is a portrait of a foppish nobleman, wearing an extraordinary multi-feathered hat, more like a woman's. Behind him are two houses (the town?), a river, trees, and in the upper corner Albrecht's sign, an "A" that is drawn very much in the manner of the Dürer "D"—all this in a print a little larger than a commemorative postage stamp. It is called, in a dim note on the back, *The Little Standard Bearer*, but there is no sign of a standard anywhere, and, in contrast to the houses and elevation on which he stands, he seems anything but little.

I am fond of the minuscule engraving, far more for its antiquity, its perfect condition after almost four hundred and fifty years, and its size—it's the smallest piece of art I own —than for its contents. Another welcome case of lessness, I suppose.

⋅

FROM ED Kessler I received an offprint of a review in the *Times Literary Supplement* of the fourth volume of Gustave Flaubert's letters. It is a very long review (three large pages of *TLS*'s four-point print) and written by a novelist I favor, Julian Barnes. He is the author of *A History of the World in 10 ½ Chap-*

ters, a superb book that belonged in my short list of notable lessness novels. His review is so long and so detailed that I felt I had read the 1,484 pages of the letters between Flaubert and George Sand without ever acquiring the book.

To Barnes, letters were often the best biography, or perhaps, he said, they constitute the best novel for a person's life. Flaubert's letters were extraordinary, as extraordinary as Sand's to him. She claimed that solitude was bad for him, and that it created a tyrannical ego. She told him "not to live in literature so much." He should go to the gym for exercise. He ought to marry. He should visit Victor Hugo.

Apparently Flaubert did pay a visit to Hugo. But he wrote to Sand that the great man did little but utter idiocies about Goethe. He wrote that the visit made him ill. . . . I liked hearing that Flaubert was a deep conservative about his writing instruments. He refused to advance from the quill pen he always used to "the newfangled steel nib," making him a fit member of the contemporary Lead Pencil Club, which pushes for that instrument in preference to the computer.

The two writers were very different. She was a social, happy, outgoing performer of a writer, he a reclusive, gloomy sort. Barnes wrote that Sand "could not disguise her distaste for the Flaubertian aesthetic. . . ." What are they each engaged on? she asked. He is surely preparing a work of "desolation," she one of "consolation."

O, I thought, this was a perfect description of the difference between my way of thinking (on the whole, desolatory) and my friend James Hillman's consolatory optimism. He has written a new book, *The Force of Character*, that describes the positive uses of old age. He believes (I am quoting from the catalog description of the book) that "even old age's debilitating changes are necessary and meaningful." He sees value in the decline of short-term memory (we then recall the past and reevaluate our lives). In his unequivocal view there is good even in the decline of physical power: "it allows us to be still and notice life's wonders."

He writes: "Aging can free you from conventional restriction and transform you into a force of nature, releasing your deepest beliefs, your passionate intensity."

When Sand told Flaubert that literature should be an act of consolation (I am again using Julian Barnes's review), he quoted to her the French lexicographer Maximilian Littre's summary of the human condition: "Man is an unstable compound and Earth a decidedly inferior planet."

Flaubert would not accept Sand's definition of literature as an act of consolation. "I cannot change my eyes," he wrote.

Nor am I able to change mine. Hillman is a sunny man, like sunny George Sand, whose intellectual and physical powers in his old age (he is seventy-three, I believe) have survived almost untouched by the usual debilities that make the last years, for so many, unpleasant, even unbearable. There are some, perhaps even many, here and there, like him. They are what Stendhal called "the happy few."

But when the body fails, and the mind weakens, and unwanted loneliness becomes the condition of life, it must be very hard to bring oneself to believe that there is meaning and positive value in it all. A deep faith may allow one to make this transfer from despair and physical misery to a state of passionate intensity that is both heartening and creative, but it is not the ordinary aged experience.

I thought of the end of Beckett's *L'Innommable*, in which the despairing but still accepting Voice is heard to say:

You must go on,
I can't go on,
I'll go on.

and the less assuring words near the end of *Waiting for Godot:*

ESTRAGON: I can't go on like this.
VLADIMIR: That's what you think.

◆

MY MIND was not entirely occupied by the dire and the dour. A few days ago I heard someone tell a story in the grocery store. It seems a tourist went to buy some lobsters and asked the fisherman how the world was treating him. The lobsterman was silent a moment. Then he said: "Seldom." This was typical of jokes told in Maine that revolved about a special, original, local, and humorous interpretation of a word or phrase, like:

A foreman in a boat-building factory was asked how many men worked there. His answer: "About half."

And the much heard but still typical joke: a Mainer was asked if he'd lived in Stonington all his life. "Not yet," he replied.

Or this: a tourist pulled up to the curb and asked a native: "Can I take this road to Bangor?" "Guess you can," the Mainer answered. "But I expect they got plenty of them up there."

I found most of these old saws in *Maine Sampler*, published thirty-five years ago by Bill Sawyer, but they are still heard today, in one form or another, whenever outlanders, or better, those from away, gather. The tone of the stories told by them is often condescending, but it shouldn't be. The sharp responses of the replies turn the joke on the foolishness of the questioner, who asks a question that is easily, quickly answered by the wit of the native.

After I wrote this, I wondered: Did these few paragraphs recording some legendary Maine stories qualify me as a Maine writer?

•

AFTER I published a book on solitude and another on private prayer I continued to read the books that Thomas Merton published (too many, he thought) on meditation, prayer, solitude. Then, in a recent letter, Margaret Whalen, my friend from the days of May Sarton, mentioned in an offhand way that Merton had had a love affair late in his life.

How had I missed the publication of his fifth journal, *Learning to Love*, that appeared more than a year ago? To take my mind off lists and invitations, I went to the excellent Blue Hill bookstore, fortunately found it in paper, and read it at once, with the kind of absorption that one gives to such revelations. For the portrait I had always had from the earlier books of a contented, isolated, deeply religious, totally out-of-the-world, sturdy monk-priest-hermit came to pieces in this journal.

Here was a man deeply in love, torn between his vows and his need for the young student-nurse, identified only as M., whom he had first encountered when he had a serious back operation in a Louisville hospital. They met only a few times, during which their love was close, even intimate, but apparently never consummated. They exchanged numerous letters and phone calls (these last from the monastery were "illegal"). Then Merton, after the most painful agonizing, chose his beloved solitude in the woods over the possible gratifications of love, marriage, and a child. In his hermitage he now found everything hard: "If only I can keep from thinking about her body maybe I can sleep. . . . "

While this was going on, he recorded in his journal all the details of his complicated life as a writer. He recognized the falsity of the portrait the world had of him through his writings. The reality of his life was bitter: he drank beer to dull his desire for M. His health was very bad, causing him to leave Gethsemani often for medical treatments for his bursitis, his painful back, his numerous allergies, his stomach troubles. On these trips he met friends at bars and restaurants, went home with them to listen to new recordings by Joan Baez, the Beatles, and Bob Dylan ("Should a hermit like Bob Dylan?" he asked plaintively), his favorite musicians, and, sometimes, philosophers.

More, he rebelled against the monastery with which the world so unquestioningly associated him. It was the abbot, Dom James, who occasioned his greatest animus: "He is a depressing and deadening force in my life, sickening, negative, sterile." Dom James censored his letters to M., and kept her letters from him. He prevented him from going to international conferences, meetings, lectures he was invited to give, thus reducing his worldly life to nothing. While Merton says this was probably good for him, his resentment creeps in: he cannot help recording every instance of this deprivation.

There was more: his occasional resentment of his monastery and, it must be said, the bureaucratic Catholic Church to which he had devoted his life. In these last years (he died two years later) he saw the church as an avatar of Kafka's *The Castle*.

It [the novel] so exactly describes life in the Catholic Church! The firm and stable unreality of relations between subject and superior—the creation of a small, pseudo-supernatural mystery world of curial bureaus from which emanate incomprehensible instructions, warnings, rewards. . . .

In another place, he added: "The book [*The Castle*] reinforces my conclusion that there is *nothing* to be looked for from Church officialdom." Whatever he accomplished in his writing was done in spite of the abbot's censorship; he began to question his own presence in the monastery: ". . . I pretend I belong here," and, he adds poignantly: ". . . as if I belonged somewhere."

Merton's literary preferences were, curiously, for William Faulkner and most of all for Albert Camus, the existential, agnostic novelist. He wrote sympathetically on Camus' questioning philosophy, especially his doubts about faith in *The Plague*. It was never clear to me what Faulkner's attraction for Merton was, but he continued to praise most of the novels unstintingly.

At the end of this journal, there is a heartrending letter to M. He said that his vowed life had to be continued. "I know I am where I belong," he said, although a little further on he wrote that he had "to find my own way, without a map . . . working it out as I go along . . . this means in fact living as an absurd kind of hermit when I am really not a hermit."

In a postscript he defines his other, and perhaps dominant vocation:

The work of writing can be for me . . . the simple job of *being*: by creative reflection and awareness to help life itself live in me. . . . For to write is to love: it is to inquire and to praise, or to confess, or to appeal. This testimony of love remains necessary. Not to reassure myself that I am ("I write therefore I am"), but simply to pay my debt to life, to the world, to other men. . . . The bad writing I have done has all been authoritarian. . . .

I learned from Merton's journal what I should have known were I not so innocent, that the monk is not a simple, symbolic figure who represents for the worldly the pure, untroubled life of prayer and meditation. Instead, he is a person like all persons. He has chosen to live apart, suffering the common demons and temptations alone, trying desperately to conquer them, to be *better*.

◆

I CONTINUED TO check off the days on my desk calendar, watching the time diminish until the first guest was due to arrive, the daughter who was bringing champagne and other necessities only obtainable from New York. The calendar reminded me of that bleak morning of December 31, 1995, when Sybil and I sat in the holding room (they termed it) of the Eastern Maine Medical Center, waiting for someone to come with papers to sign, papers that made sure she knew the responsibility was hers should she succumb during bypass surgery.

I had studied the wall where there hung a sign that declared, in bold black letters: **TODAY   IS**   and nothing more. The blank space was disconcerting, almost ominous. I said nothing to Sybil, who was nervous enough as it was, but I found myself composing Beckettian lines:

1:	What day is today?
SOME OTHER:	What does it say?
1:	It says no day.
SOME OTHER:	So that's the day it is.
1:	I see.

A nurse came for Sybil to take her to the cardiac unit. I gathered up our coats and went to the waiting room, reserved for those waiting to hear about the outcome of cardiac operations. I found a copy of the *Wall Street Journal* and looked at the heading. It was Friday.

◆

IT WAS a very long wait. I had brought a copy of *The American Scholar* with me and read an article about the composer Virgil Thompson. He said of the city of Paris when he was a student there that "nothing seemed to be going on because everything was going on," and so it seemed to me that long day at the end of December and the year. I kept looking at my watch and the hands never seemed to move. I had Primo Levi's *The Periodic Table* with me to reread. Early into it, I came upon a description of Sandro, who "didn't like watches: he felt their quiet continuous admonition to be an arbitrary intrusion." Yes. I took mine off and put it in my jacket pocket. . . . Then I found myself looking constantly at the clock on the wall.

I remember that sometime during the wait I went to the cafeteria for lunch. The food, like the food in all hospital cafeterias, was terrible. I was pleased I had brought along the Virgil Thompson article to read. He said he went to Paris in 1925 because he "preferred to starve where the food was good." O for Paris now.

Five hours and sixteen minutes later I learned the operation was a success.

◆

I DREADED BECOMING eighty in a few weeks, as much as I had dreaded being seventy, and sixty. But now I feared being asked how I accounted for my relative longevity and I had no answer for it except to repeat my dislike of being asked to account for it. I wanted to think of something clever, like Sir Basil Blackwell's response when he reached ninety. He said he came to this milestone by "being in a constant state of mild irritation." . . . And Ted Nowick reported of his mother, who, when asked to account for her longevity (she lived to be ninety-nine), replied: "I never learned to drive."

◆

I wondered why I had even thought to celebrate a time that I disliked so much. But there was Sybil, who loved parties and had offered to give a dinner at a restaurant in town for the people from away, on the night before the tent event on Saturday.

There was Sybil to celebrate. We had been together for twenty-five years, a union that once was regarded as *scandaleux* but, in the current climate for such odd couples, seemed to be accepted by most persons. I have always regarded the homosexual life as an extension of, not a change from, heterosexuality. I did not "come out" violently, I moved on, from a happy thirty years with a husband I loved and with whom I led a most satisfactory sexual life, to a new mode, a new experience, a new love that now has lasted almost as long as my marriage.

A genuine lesbian union is, in every sense except the legal, a marriage. For us, the domestic life has been no different from what our former arrangements were, except that perhaps there is more commonality, more equality, fewer unshared tasks. There are the same obligations and responsibilities to each other. We adhere to the words of the marriage ceremony: "to have and to hold until death do us part" without ever having recited them in church or judge's chambers. We live the words of another form as well: to "love her, comfort her, honor her and keep her, in sickness and in health; and, forsaking all others, be faithful to her as long as you both shall live." These are sacramental words that we have never uttered, but we live as if we had. We obey these injunctions without ever having sworn to them.

Strangely enough, in every one of my novels I have written about the homosexual experience, but never have I put down explicitly the details of our union. Sybil has moved in and out of my five memoirs, sometimes identified as "S.," sometimes by name, but I never made clear her importance in every move and decision of my life. Often when I wrote I used the first-person-singular pronoun to describe an event in our lives when the truth would have required the first-person plural. Always she hoped she wouldn't appear in the books at all, that I "would leave her out."

I think her omission from much of my writing is not at her command but because a union such as ours is lived out in the wider context of the social fabric. It is not the end-all and be-all of our mutual existence, a purely sexual matter that so much lesbian fiction seems to suggest, but part of whole lives that encompass our careers, our friends and separate families, our lives as lovers of music and literature and art and travel and the beautiful places we have been lucky enough to live in: everything that characterizes more conventional unions.

I was fortunate, I thought, as we sat down one evening to plan the seating at her dinner. I had a good friend who wanted to give a party for me, a good companion, a beloved woman with whom to face the terror of coming into the end zone, the inevitable advances into the unfamiliar places of old age.

◆

W E H A D been looking at some old movies of Sybil's family. A niece had pieced together a video from disparate home movies, most of them at least fifty-five years old. There were black-and-white short shots of children at play on a beach, adults on fishing vacations. The children mug, wave, advance self-consciously toward the camera, laughing inexplicably, clearly embarrassed and not knowing what to do with their bodies and their hands, giving the artificial appearance of vitality as they pretend to pull each other into the water. The adults greet an unknown (to us) person in front of the hotel their father owned. Charles Lindbergh, Sara Roosevelt, guests of the hotel, make brief appearances, but there are many unidentified persons on the film.

Old home movies: they bore the uninitiated spectator. But are they not important records, however incomplete and brief, of lives once lived and now almost forgotten, of children now become aged adults, of places once loved or visited? Their significance as captured memory struck me especially, for my family was recorded only on worn, cracked, and yellowed photographs whose date and place I could only guess at. And worse, there was among them photographs of persons I cannot recognize, ladies with great bosoms and even larger hats wrapped in tippets of anonymous fur, men with bowler hats, enormous mustaches, and hair parted precisely in the middle. Who were these persons from my past? How have they managed to slip from my memory? And if I cannot identify them, have I lost a part of myself? This led me to wonder, as Beckett would: who, then, am I?

◆

IN THE *Washington Post* yesterday I read an account of the tribulations of those who have been forced from the welfare rolls and into meager jobs with no health insurance. They are now leading worse lives than before, but at least, ironically, the government is no longer supporting them. Many of them are single women with children to care for, or disabled or retarded persons. I remembered that Franklin Delano Roosevelt spoke out on the subject in his 1938 Annual Message to Congress (as it was then called). Luckily, I was able to locate it in a history of those years:

> Government has a final responsibility for the welfare of its citizens. If private cooperative effort fails to provide work for willing hands and relief for the unfortunate, those suffering hardship through no fault of their own have a right to call upon the government for aid. And a government worthy of the name must make a fitting response.

This no longer seemed to be the case. Everything is different since it changed, and not in any sense for the better.

I mourned this backward progress, a sad oxymoron, but a true description of the way political thought has advanced.

Later that evening I listened to National Public Radio and, to my further dismay, heard that a contest was being held nationwide for grammar school students. They were asked to write and illustrate their own stories. The winner would receive, not the complete works of Shakespeare, or of Jane Austen, or the King James Bible, suitably inscribed to the winner, not any of those that were awarded for academic achievement in my youth, but instead, a computer.

Robert Frost has his oven bird ask, "What to make of a diminished thing." I found myself asking this of "progress." During my reading of the cycle of Psalms I came upon other writings, here and there, bearing on what the Psalms led me to be aware of:

Pascal, in *Pensées:* "It is the heart which perceives God and not the reason."

Mendel of Kotzk (cited in Martin Buber, *Tales of the Hasidim*): "God dwells wherever man lets him in."

Emily Dickinson: "They say that God is everywhere, and yet we always think of Him as something of a recluse."

1 Corinthians, 3: 18–19: "For the wisdom of this world is the foolishness of God."

The *Talmud*: "God wants the heart."

W. R. Inge, found in *The Oxford Book of Aphorisms:* "Many people believe they are attracted by God or by Nature when they are only repelled by Man." This might well have been written by Mark Twain.

Rabbi Abraham Herschel: "Our awareness of God communes with the ineffable beyond us."

Leon Wieseltier (*Kaddish*): "The rabbi gave me a key to the shul. Now I can come early or stay late. I have a haven. *I like being alone with my religion*" (my italics). . . . In shul among the early-morning worshipers: "I am in a gathering of genuinely religious people. All the other explanations for what they are doing here are moot. Their faith is an irreducible quantum. They are here because they believe, and I am here because they believe."

Wieseltier again: "The notion that I am essentially spirit may be preposterous, but the notion that I am essentially flesh is more preposterous."

In a book I loved when I was young, *Anne of Green Gables*, the heroine says, wisely for a little girl: "Saying one's prayers is not the same as praying." This piece of young wisdom touched peripherally upon two of my beliefs, that prayer is not solely a matter of formal words and phrases, and that they do not need to be spoken. Astute little Anne.

◆

I HAVE ALWAYS read the obituaries in the *New York Times*, both the extended ones under black headlines and the privately placed ones in tiny type. In the harassed days before I reached eighty I found that I read them even more closely. I used to think that I paid attention to them in order to feel superior; after all, one had survived even the featured dead. But yesterday, reading the dread page, I discovered a better reason for turning first to the obituaries every day. I was reading about persons who were notable enough in their lives to merit lengthy considerations at their death but of whom I had never heard.

Today, for example, Woody Stephens, eighty-four, a Hall of Fame horse trainer, died. For him there was a two-column write-up. Mourners of other notable persons, no doubt fearing that no such extended notice will be taken of their death, sometimes submit to the newspaper at some cost, I would imagine, extended two-point notices, some a column long. Here are to be found descriptions of the lives of unsung physicians, philanthropists, teachers, scholars, businessmen, politicians, all of whose deaths are reduced to tiny print with no headlines.

Who at the newspaper decides to grant a day of enlarged fame to a horse trainer, another day to a rap singer, and another to a Mafia boss, and sentence all the others who died at about the same time to printed obscurity? I have noticed that, occasionally, the editors of that page are pressured, by the continued appearance of a short but detailed obituary, to elevate that person to full treatment. This does not happen often, for fame in death, even for a day, is as chancy, it would seem, as it is in life, and liable to the vagaries of editorial choice.

◆

Sybil and I engaged in a running game of gin rummy. We no longer played for money but for fun and for glory. When I mixed the cards I saw my mother's hands in mine, hers, however, those of a youthful, excellent card player, and my old, veined, spotted hands a sadly reduced version of hers.

◆

The grass on the lawn, and the sections of it in the meadow, seemed greener than usual. The men who had laid the new patio, and put down green sod around its edges, had finally departed. We sat on the deck picturing the patio peopled by our guests at the party having their drinks and canapés out there. We observed how lucky we were that this project, one of Sybil's most fortunate ideas, was finished in time for the event, and that, contrary to the adage, the grass was greener close by.

After Sybil had gone to work across the way at the bookstore, I stayed on the deck, thinking about how foolishly devoted I was to this place, to the acres of scrabbly woods, lawn, meadow, the garden circle we had made, Sybil's rock garden that I took very occasional care of, and the cove that provided me with all the varieties of color, form, and light I will ever need. It seemed strange that after only ten years of living here, my roots were so deep. I felt somewhat disconnected to other long-term places in my life: the cement of Manhattan, where I was born and grew up and went to college, Des Moines, upstate New York, Washington, D.C.

The popples (local name for poplars) and scrub maples, the few slender, strong birches, and the two "major" trees, a majestic horse chestnut that dominates the lawn, and the distant oak near the water: these composed the essential landscape of my life. Every rock (there are two huge ones on our front lawn, another the anchor of the new patio) held down parts of my psychic scenery. These roots, these downward ties are what held me irrevocably to this place, the *Plas Newydd* (as the Ladies of Llangollen called their beloved home), the New Place, the fortress of my old age.

There was, of course, the house, the place we have added to, enlarged the study, strengthened the windows, built a room that serves as library, and a garage that is connected to the house, in true Maine style, by a small room called by Sybil "the hyphen." I have always thought we should have celebrated these changes and additions by some ancient rites. Tracy Kidder in his marvelous account, *House*, says the anthropologist Mircea Eliade believed that sacrifices at the new foundations of buildings "stemmed from a once widespread conviction that a building had to be animated. If it was going to stand and endure, a construction needed life."

Our more than hundred-year-old house with its additions I regard as a construction not unlike the Puritan view of houses (again I take this from Kidder), "human imitations of divine handiwork. A roof was like a head, rafters were like bones, posts were shoulders, clapboards were skin, windows were eyes, doors were mouths, a threshold was lips, and a chimney was the breast in which lay the heart, which resembled the hearth, which contained the flame, which stood for the soul."

Like the Puritans I thought of our house as built "to the standards God used in constructing the human body." It seemed to me a living, breathing being, enclosing in its arms our family that now included a cat. Its interior space was divided into chambers, like the heart. To leave it would be like deserting a person one had promised to care for. I could not conceive of doing that.

◆

SYBIL CAME back to the house to deliver two E-mail letters (is that a tautology?) to me and told me she was sure that the favorite name for a female baby in the twenty-first century would be Dotcom.

◆

THE CLIMATE in the house, when I was there alone in the long hours of the day, was silence. For some mysterious reason both the chimes and the ticking of the grandfather clock have ceased, and the discreet, introverted cat, so far, has made no noise. I know that the furnace, and the washing machine, and the refrigerator made some noise, but without my hearing aids I did not notice them. I enjoyed the absence of all sound. But sometimes I found myself listening for the silence. When I seemed to hear it, it expanded the walls of my study as if they were a balloon. It stopped up the canals of my inner ears so that I was only aware of matters that emanated from the inside of me, no-sound making room for them.

Ash Wednesday (T. S. Eliot)

Against the Word the unstilled World still whirled
About the center of the silent Word.

Sometimes, like the autumn in Thomas Hood's poem, I stand "shadowless like silence, listening to Silence." I wondered if, in my old age, I was becoming mad, listening for what was not there, not hearing it, and then delighting in its absence.

◆

WHILE I relished the view of low hills and the lack of buildings in the view Billings Cove afforded me, I sometimes missed two high structures I had grown to love in Washington: the Capitol, resplendent in sunset light, and the Washington Monument. In the night sky two small lights shone in the obelisk's triangular top that, to my eyes, made it look rather like a sheet-clad Ku Klux Klansman.

But when I remembered the shaft of the monument I thought of the story I once read about its opening in 1888. It then contained a steam elevator to take visitors to the top. Considered a very dangerous machine, only men were allowed to use it; women, poor souls, who wished to ascend the monument were required to climb the 698 steps and then come down again on foot. They were only admitted to the elevator eighty years later when the stairway itself was deemed dangerous—a few persons were injured by reaching out to the elevator from the stairs—and was closed. I loved this story of the curiously turned-about requirement for women, which I found in Bryson B. Rash's humorous book of anecdotes about Washington, D.C.

◆

I TRIED, AGAIN and again, in the weeks before the party, to work on the unfinished novel. It had been in a drawer for many years while I finished and published other books. I thought of it as a constant. Why did I keep going back to it? I thought of Ivy Compton-Burnett's remark about writing: "What a difficult work to choose! But of course one did not choose it. There was no choice." Perhaps it's also true that it chose us, very early, and never let go of us. About finding usable material for her novels, she said to a friend (this is quoted in Hilary Sperling's excellent life of the quirky writer), "We have to dig it out of our insides . . . something's there trying to get out. . . . It's sort of trying to get out and wants help."

I had the first section of the novel typed out. The last three paragraphs had been written first, as is my custom; the rest was in my head. Virginia Woolf once wrote, somewhere (I could not find it in all her published letters and diaries), that she had just written a short story. All that remained was to put it down on paper.

Yes. Getting it on paper was the trick. While the book was still in my head it always seemed so good, so perfect in content, design, and tone. Then something happened. During the journey from the memory cells of the brain to the fingers, the trip to the tip of the pen, and thence to the paper, the ideal was usually lost. I stared down at scrabbly, imperfect, unsatisfactory pages. They had suffered a serious, inevitable decline. I needed to start again, perhaps to engage in a new itinerary, like digging it out of my insides.

◆

OUR KITTEN was fast becoming a cat. She seemed more judgmental than before, looking at me severely as if to register genuine disapproval when I worked at my desk and dissatisfaction with the content of her meals. In a letter to William Maxwell, the novelist Silvia Townsend Warner told him that her three cats drove her crazy when she had flu, "gazing at me with large eyes & saying: O Silvia, you are so ill, you'll soon be dead.

And who will feed us then? *Feed us now!*" Jean-Isabel McNutt recounts this story in her commonplace book, *Echoes of Eden.*

◆

To ADD to fretting over the details of the parking problem for the party—how will all those cars fit into our driveway and circle, even taking into account the parking lot of the bookstore?—I received two letters from an elderly reader complaining about the despondent character of my writing about old age. She told me I was mistaken, that there were positive joys in that state, among them a new kind of freedom she had never experienced before, freedom from worries about others, freedom from family routines and husband-demands (I assume she was a widow), freedom from the daily demands of meals, care of clothing, housecleaning. This was a happy time of life, she insisted, that I did not properly recognize.

It was true, I acknowledged. That is, it was true for her, and the few who live on into the usually bleak land of old age without bodily afflictions or mental decline. (She did not mention freedom from pain or suffering.)

But then, some time later, I was forced to reconsider my absolutist views about the state of mind of even those who found contentment in what had always seemed to me unpleasant conditions of the last years. I received a letter from Hetty Archer, a friend who had moved from her beloved home in Maine to an assisted-living apartment in Portland (Oregon) to be near her son. Despite her wretched scleroderma, which continued to worsen, she was cheerful about her residence and her condition. She even saw some advantages to them. "Now that I'm eighty, it's easier to portion out my energy." She acknowledged that, in the place she was in, "everyone here copes with some misery, [so] we understand each other and enjoy swapping advice and even find humor in some earthy situations."

She was a woman who loved animals, especially strays. She wrote that an old tomcat had walked into her living room and settled on her couch. She and her two elderly dogs adopted him. She had to build a small porch on her backyard patio because Tom angered the neighbors by yowling at the moon and pooping in their flower boxes; otherwise, Tom added to her contentment.

> So I've slowed down, reluctantly at first, then time began to stretch out and it is just lovely to sit in my lazy-girl chair, animals on me or nearby, in a more or less comatose state. There are small breaks, like a meal, a phone call, dogs to let out, then bring them in, a call of nature (too damn often), a snooze, a book (for effect), perhaps a pony of Kahlua.

And in another place she wrote: "Life is simpler now that everything is slowing down: peristalsis, recall, sex, proper responses, simple math, reactions to frustrations. . . . Things that used to drive me crazy have lost importance. I have learned how happy I can be just keeping warm and my feet up."

And she concluded with an admirable effusion: "I am the luckiest woman in the world. What an incredible century. What a wild and woolly country. What a god-awful world."

So much for my cheerless view of the afflictions and displacements of age. Beckett and Yeats thought it was a time to rage against. I too. But not Hetty Archer.

◆

Browsing in the bookstore, I came upon a copy of an issue of a magazine called *The Little Review*, Margaret Anderson, publisher and editor, as stated on the cover. Its subhead was "A Magazine of the Arts." The date of this issue was 1917, but I believe it was founded a few years earlier.

What I admired most about the small publication was the statement of intention written in tiny capital letters on the cover: "MAKING NO COMPROMISE WITH PUBLIC TASTE." Imagine a magazine today making such an announcement. It was most unlikely, after its inevitable months of "market research," to find out exactly what the public wanted. Emphasizing that courageous declaration was the inclusion of a piece by Ezra Pound (who is listed on the cover as "Foreign Editor") entitled "L'Homme Moyen Sensual" and another by T. S. Eliot, "Eeldrop and Appleplex" (certainly not titles designed to attract reader interest), and signed, I'm sure to the author's and the proofreader's dismay, T. *H*. Eliot.

The publication moved to Paris and began to publish Ernest Hemingway (before fame became of him), Robert McAlmon, and Gertrude Stein. It lasted about seven more years, and went down for financial reasons, I think. Or perhaps it was because its insistence on not compromising with public taste did it in.

◆

I WAS IMPRESSED by the catholicity of our cat's views on the proper place to sleep. I have strict requirements: my own large bed placed so that I can see the cove, feather pillows, a down quilt, and an electric blanket to warm the bed before I enter it. Not KK. She will sleep in any place in the house that is soft. At night she often settles into a site that allows her commanding views of our bedrooms and the bathroom. In this way she will be aware of all our movements: she is a faithful nocturnal sentinel. During the day she prefers comfortable places in sunlight, or under the light over my computer in a box of discarded manuscript. Sybil believes she considers this a beach. She is sunning herself in cool Maine's version of the Caribbean.

◆

Samuel Beckett called upon writers to violate all the strenuous efforts I made every day for exactness of word, phrase, sentence, meaning. "The most real element in the fiction you write will be the uncertainty." I thought perhaps his secret was to accomplish this by strict limitation upon the prose, thus allowing for doubt while certainty was somehow an underlying suggestion. Did this duality satisfy the reader?

The ending of mystery stories, with every situation firmly resolved, is always very satisfying and probably (I do not know for certain for I never wrote one) not too difficult to bring off. But serious fiction often ends in ambiguity, leaving the reader feeling uneasy, even angry. Why not resolve everything? Doesn't the writer know how it ends? Ah, but life is full of vagueness, unsolved puzzles and situations, and eventually, an uncertain conclusion.

◆

To help us decide where to hold the first dinner party we went to sample the food at The Landing, a rather fancy, not to say pretentious and pricey restaurant in Brooksville with a fine view of the yachts in Buck's Harbor. We took our friend Helen Yglesias with us so that we could taste three choices on the menu.

The owner-hostess and waitress, who knew our intent, were unusually attentive to us, although on a previous, anonymous visit this was not so, and the chef in full regalia came out to assure us that he would prepare some fine dishes for our guests. We ate a very good dinner, it was true. But "ate" was the wrong verb. I recalled Maurice Chevalier saying: "I never eat when I can dine." In the end we decided not to dine there for the party because it was too out-of-the-way for the people staying in Blue Hill and hard to find for some others.

◆

At three-thirty in the morning I lay in bed worrying, about everything. My latest concern: where will everybody eat breakfast on Saturday? One worry always opened the gates to new ones. I went off in another direction and began to worry about my lack of creative ideas and my absorption with foolish detail in my daily life. At about four I had come to the conclusion that at the end of one's life new ideas are very rare. It is seldom one becomes what Auden said Freud was in his old age, "a climate of opinion."

◆

Would it rain for the party? July was often a wet month in Maine, and the chance of rain was good. There is nothing more futile than worrying about the weather. Yet this realization did not prevent me from anxiety. Such disquiet is common, I have discovered, on the continent of old age: old persons worried about everything, including what we could do nothing about.

In youth, all one's experiences were unique, colorful, full of possibilities, and we fretted about none of them. As we aged, our lives and our identities narrowed. We grew more and more alike. We shared much of the same disappointments, anxieties, cares, pains, despairs. At first we considered them only our own. But a conversation with another aged citizen revealed their commonality. We were limited by dreary subject matter: the state of our health, our memory lapses, the deaths of our friends, our own problematic survival, the terrible, retrogressive condition of the world in general and in particular. We grew to be clones of each other and, as Emerson wrote, we all contracted the extent of the "firmament/ To compass of a tent."

But then I remembered Hetty, who found consolation in these similarities. She had temporarily lifted my spirits, although after a time my customary doubts began to set in: I would never be able to achieve her cheerful acceptance. Or John Cowper Powys' ungrudging compromise: in *The Art of Growing Old* he wrote: "We poor dullards of habit and custom . . . require the hell of a flaming thunderbolt to rouse us to the fact *that every single second of conscious life is a miracle past reckoning* . . . " (my italics).

♦

I N T H E crowded days before the party I managed, temporarily, to put my worries to rest by reading Thomas Merton's seventh and final *Journal.* For someone constantly in search of titles suggesting the state of one's mind or age, I thought that Father Patrick Hart, the editor of this volume, chose a good one: *The Other Side of the Mountain*, a phrase used by Merton as he looked at a mountain outside his window in Tibet.

The *Journal* has all the elements of tragedy, not limited to the fact that a few days after the last entry Merton was accidentally electrocuted in his cottage room on the outskirts of Bangkok.

For the first time since he took his vows as a monk twenty-seven years before, Merton had been free to travel, a more liberal and sympathetic abbot having been elected in his monastery. The places he visited, to give lectures and participate in conferences and forums, became, in this journal, sites he considered as possible refuges from Gethsemini. He realized he needed to find an escape from the noise, busyness, and constant stream of visitors to his hermitage.

He looked for the solitude he required in California, in Alaska. But it was not only that his fame as a writer had made his hermitage uninhabitable for him. He wrote that he had always felt a stranger in the monastery he had lived in for all of his adult life, and to which he had brought worldwide fame. He echoed the novelist Brian Moore, who wrote: "I am an exile from everywhere." In his earlier journal, Merton had been tempted to leave because of his love for a young woman; in this one he looked back at that long, temptation-filled year as misguided and foolish.

Merton wondered, at the last, if he would be able to find sanctuary and solitude in India. But he was a man ridden by ambiguity. He wrote to Father Hart, two days before his death, that he missed Gethsemini, especially as Christmas was approaching. God, in His ironic way, saw to it that he found his final refuge at last in death, and that his homesickness and his exile ended where he had wished. His body was returned to Kentucky and buried in the abbey church at Gethsemini, where his journey had started, in time for Christmas.

◆

ONCE AGAIN I began to reread Tracy Kidder's absorbing account of how a house was built, from the moment a couple decided they want to live on a piece of land they have bought from her father to the day they moved into the completed house. What sent me back to Kidder? The announcement by our good friend Bill Henderson that he was in the process of building a tower on Christie Hill, an elevation not far from us.

A tower? Why a tower? Bill was vague about his motive, except to suggest that he wanted to be able to sit at the top and command a three-hundred-and-sixty-degree view of the country. Then, he thought, he would sit up there and write a book about building a tower. Only about this tower? I asked. We were now on the second bottle of red wine, and I was feeling fine, my post-herpetic pain forgotten. I mentioned Yeats, and brought out my first edition of *The Tower*. I thought about Robinson Jeffers, and Vita Sackville-West, who I remembered had written in a tower at Sissinghurst Castle at Cranbrook. I thought of some trite examples. Pisa? Eiffel?

But most of my suggestions were literary and I could tell by his response that he was thinking of many others. He said his faith (he did not explain this further) and his defiance of his fear of vertigo entered into his decision to build it. He promised to take us to the tower's foundation when the road was cleared to it.

In bed I mulled over the idea. A tower as aspiration, a visible reaching toward God? as opposed to the usual one- or two-story house that clings, agnostically, to the ground? A yearning for privacy and escape? Bill had built a cabin for his family deep in the Deer Isle woods. For the same reason? I wondered. I could come up with a few other psychological possibilities, including the obvious sexual allusion to the shape of the structure (as I imagined it would be), but that was entirely unsatisfactory. I decided to wait for Bill's book to better inform me of his intentions.

◆

Building, in any form, has always been of interest to me, ever since I worked on the *Architectural Forum* in the early forties. It came about in this way. There was an opening for someone to write building news for that august and glossy publication, so I moved over from the research team at *Time* to perform the lowly task. I think the opening was the result of the loss to the draft and then to the war of men who would ordinarily have occupied the post. After the first few issues I was given the title of associate editor, together with Peter Blake, a young architect awaiting his call from the draft, with whom I shared an office.

The job lacked substance. I read press releases and the business sections of newspapers to make building news items out of them. On two occasions I was elevated to a higher plane: I was given books to review, one by Frank Lloyd Wright, another by a completely unknown writer named Ayn Rand, whose novel was said to be based on the career of the famed architect Louis Sullivan.

Of the first I was properly reverential. But on Ayn Rand I brought to bear all the weight of my youthful, highbrow scorn. I declared *The Fountainhead* to be a terrible novel and the author an entirely untalented writer. I excoriated its libertarian, almost fascistic intellectual underpinnings. The book went on to become a best-seller. It is selling still in paperback after almost sixty years and at enormous prices in rare-book stores—but my view of its contents remains the same on all counts.

My only regret (as a book collecter and bookseller) is that I marked up the pages of my copy with a furious, thick pencil, discarded the dust jacket, and, in the end, discarded the book into the wastebasket, an act I took to be properly symbolic. If I had kept my copy in its original, pristine state, dust jacket and all, a first-edition review slip therein, it would now garner me somewhere close to two thousand dollars. So much for critical gestures.

At the *Forum* I was surrounded by notable editors: Howard Myers, an amiable and patient bear of a man who ran the magazine well; Henry Wright, the first city planner to suggest inner-city, non-traffic areas and the designer of unique, movable and multifunctional walls for apartments as well as a pioneer in energy conservation; and George Nelson, a celebrated designer of furniture and every sort of household furnishing.

Most important to me personally was the skilled architect Paul Grotz, an émigré from Germany and lately art editor of *Fortune*. He became a good friend of Frank Lloyd Wright and art editor of the *Forum*. Like almost every woman who ever met this charming, good-looking, talented man, I fell in love with him. Though I saw him rarely in the years to come, I maintained my deep affection for him until he died a few years ago. Indeed my warm feelings for him are with me still, the way love endures when it is not put to the test of proximity and dailiness. The old saying is true of love: " 'Tis distance lends enchantment to the view."

There was Maddie Thatcher, Paul Grotz's assistant, a quiet, competent draftswoman who was the first dedicated Christian Scientist I had ever met. I was always riddled with late-adolescent allergies and colds; she of course was never sick. I remember that she once lent me a copy of Mary Baker Eddy's *Science and Health with Key to the Scriptures*, which I started to read earnestly in hope of some cures. But I had to abandon it because of the unreadable quality of the prose.

In the first year at the *Forum*, and for the second time in my short life, I came, in a humorous sort of way, close to greatness. Peter Blake had been a tutor to Bertrand Russell's young son, Conrad, in England. When Russell was invited by Albert

Barnes to lecture at his house in Merion, Pennsylvania, Peter and I once met him at the station on his return to the city and took him to his hotel in New York, where he stayed until it was time to give his Rand lecture in the city.

The manager at the Lafayette, at Tenth Street in Greenwich Village, seemed delighted to welcome Lord Russell. I remember watching him sign the register with a flourish and wondered if he were being accorded free privileges. It was probably not so, because after our drinks at a marble-topped table in the coffee shop, we went upstairs to Russell's room, a tiny cell of a place without a private bath.

When Peter went down the long hall to the men's room, I was alone with Russell. The seventy-two-year-old philosopher closed the door, pushed me down on the bed, opened the buttons of his fly, and climbed atop of me. He was a small but amazingly virile chap. Fortunately, by the time he had succeeded in reaching through the layers of my clothes, Peter had returned and interrupted the proceedings.

Russell was most nonchalant at being interrupted, Peter pretended not to notice as the great man closed his buttons and I, much relieved, rearranged my skirt and sweater. We said good night to Russell, he to us (I think I remember he kissed us both sedately on the cheek), and we left. As we walked down the stairs I thought, I remember clearly: this is as close as I am ever likely to come to having sex with a Nobel Prize winner.

Were he not irrevocably beyond reach, Paul Grotz was another guest I would have invited to the party. Still, in the company of the other ghosts of those past years, he may well be there.

✦

THE SUBJECT of towers continued to interest me. Was I right about Sackville-West? On my shelf I found a volume of letters between Vita and her husband, Harold Nicolson. In it was a photograph of her tower and the huge second-floor window at which she wrote. . . . Inevitably, when I have a book in hand, I meander from the main point of my search. I started to reread the letters. Four hours later I was still there, living with them their curious, admirable lives.

Harold was visiting elderly W. Somerset Maugham at Cap Ferrat in France. Willy and his companion, Gerald Haxton, led a life of luxury and the "delights of the body": swimming, sailing, sunning, and sympathetic in a way to the territorial ambitions of Adolf Hitler (it was 1938). The Duke and Duchess of Windsor came to dinner. Harold pictured perfectly to Vita the tragic couple. The Duke kept referring to his wife as Her Royal Highness although that title had been denied her by the present king. "It is pathetic the way he is sensitive about her," Harold writes, but "one cannot get away from his glamour and his charm and his sadness."

In two paragraphs four persons were sketched in with great skill. I saw them clearly. And it is the same with his portrait of Dame Ethel Smyth, the well-known composer and suffragette, who was eighty and "quite biffed" when Harold met her at a luncheon. In a few vivid sentences he described for Vita the stone-deaf old lady and her "whole wad of untidy grey hair" who carried around a headphone turned the wrong way and blew her nose into her muffler in place of her handkerchief.

Harold's view of the American ambassador to England in 1940, whom he calls "Jo Kennedy," was that he was dangerous, "a stupid man but he has a swollen head and thinks he can play a great part in world politics." In many other places, with sure depictive strokes, Harold seemed to be almost as good a fiction writer as his novelist wife.

But Vita's letters, while not as full or as interesting as Harold's, contain some wonderful assertions about their life together. "I am thinking to myself. . . . How queer. I suppose Hadji [her name for Harold] and I have been about as unfaithful to one another as one well could be from the conventional point of view, even worse than unfaithful if you add in homosexuality, and yet I swear no two people could love one another more than we do after all these years." And she adds: "It is queer, isn't it? It does destroy all orthodox ideas of marriage," and finally, "I do think we have managed things cleverly."

By means of all this good rereading I had strayed easily, delightedly, from the idea of tower. What I looked for and found eventually was Vita's description of the use of her tower in the early years of the war: "Beale . . . wanted to inspect the country from the top of the tower. . . . It was not only parachutists they are afraid of but troop-carrying planes landing on our own Sissinghurst fields. . . ."

Vita later visited another tower in Essex, Layer Marney, an eight-story Tudor brick tower, the tallest in England, which stands beside a little church. I went to my desk to write to Bill to tell him about this latest discovery, and to alert him to another possible tower for use in his book. Who knows? In the next war his may be commandeered to serve as watchtower for enemy landings in Sargentville.

◆

EARLY LETTERS of congratulation came from two former colleagues at American University. I hadn't heard from them in many years. It had nothing to do with their kind remembrance of me, but suddenly I was reminded of the reasons why I de-

cided to leave academe. They were both frivolous, even somewhat humorous. It was late spring. I was driving on a road
within the campus and perhaps inadvertently occupying too
much of the narrow space when a male student thrust his head
out of his window and shouted "Asshole!" All the long, careful
decorum, the *politesse* between student and professor crashed
with that word. This was a new generation, one in the driver's
seat or better, now sitting in President Grayson Kirk's chair at
Columbia University, smoking his cigars. . . .

And a few days later, after an interminable four hours at an
English department meeting, during which nothing was resolved and every possible variant upon the subject had been expressed by everyone present, a faculty member rose and said:
"It is all a matter of semantics."

I could not recall a meeting at which I had not heard that
sentiment expressed. But this time it was too much. I held my
two last classes, returning papers, wishing the students well,
said good-bye. Without a word to my colleagues, I packed up
my books, cleared out my desk, took down a Hogarth print
from the wall, and made three trips to my car in a distant parking lot. I wrote a note to the chairman of the department and
left it on his desk. Using the long-distance line of the university
for the last time, I put through a call to the office of the teachers' insurance plan in New York and activated my retirement
pension.

It was a month before my sixty-fourth birthday. After thirty
years of teaching I retired into full-time writing, where, ironically, it all became a matter of semantics.

◆

Two letters from readers came today. Both suggested a title for memoirs were I to engage in another such enterprise:

Leftovers. Overtime. A few days ago someone offered me *Time Out.* I thought about them. Titles are an interesting subject, because once I have settled on one for a book, it is hard for me to change it. It has hardened absolutely into marquee reality. Even if the suggested replacement (by the editor, by the sales manager) is better than mine, more accurate, or more likely to catch the eye of the prospective buyer, it seems impossible for me to adopt another one.

I remember that once I wanted to give a novel a title from words by Emily Dickinson, *Fear a Door.* It was at a time when a best-seller had been published called *Jaws.* One of my daughters, hoping for similar great success for me, suggested I call the novel *Fear a Shark.* I rejected the possibility and thus, perhaps, lost my one chance for fame and fortune.

◆

A FEW YEARS ago, Bill Henderson bestowed on me a modicum of literary fame by naming me a founder of his Lead Pencil Club, a society dedicated to the opposition of technology. We were to be the first Leadites after our Luddite predecessors. Our slogan was "Simplify, simplify," first urged upon humanity by the founder-emeritus, Henry Thoreau, and later by those masters of prose style William Strunk Jr. and E. B. White. The Club was known as "A Pothole on the Information Highway," and we advised everyone to stay with the lead pencil as the preferred mode of communication.

So this longtime member of the club suffered a shock the other day. I sat down to make yet another list of people to whom to send maps of the roads to our house and to the places in which they were to stay. To distract myself from the task I picked up a copy of the *London Review of Books* and started an ar-

ticle about the Unabomber, Theodore Kaczynski. Brian Rot-
man wrote that he was clearly mad, he was a Luddite carried
into madness during his "holy war against technology."

◆

LAST NIGHT the telephone rang. It was for me, oddly
enough. My phone number is not listed. The unknown man
gave me his first name, and told me I would receive one hundred gallons of free gas at the station of my choice if I joined the
Field and Stream Club. I inquired what the club did. He began
to describe all the fishing and hunting equipment I would be
able to purchase at discount. At this point I broke in upon his
flow of offers.

"I am eighty years old," I said.

There was a long pause during which he seemed to be absorbing this startling information, or perhaps trying to com-
prehend so advanced an age.

"Oh, lady, I'm sorry," he said and hung up.

◆

SYBIL AND I sat at the kitchen table making seating plans
(yet again) for the restaurant dinner. As I watched her, I
thought about how fortunate I was to have a friend who served
all the purposes of my life—confidante, companion, supporter
and occasional severe critic of my work, and agreeable partner
in whatever I want to do. I remembered May Sarton complaining to me when she had grown old and became ill that her life
had been taken away from her. Knowing of all the supportive
persons who moved in and out of her house, I expressed surprise that this should be so. To illustrate her point, she named
her gardener, her daily caretakers, her literary executor, lawyer

and accountant, her agent, editor, and biographer, her secretary, her live-in companion.

"I have lost control of my life," she said, "and now I need a driver. I can't drive anymore," she added as though that were the final indignity. I understood her plight, in a way. But I thought of my own good luck in this respect. Most of those co-opting (as May considered them) roles were filled for me by one beloved person who has not taken control of my life. She shares it; my autonomy is still intact. I do not have to worry about a biographer or a secretary. I've simplified, I thought, and looked over with unspoken appreciation at Sybil.

◆

By chance, Sybil found among her papers the typescript of a piece of autobiography by Luree Miller, our friend who would, perforce, be absent from the July events. She had written about the strong and long-lived women in her family. Her mother had gone back to college to study art when Luree was in her teens, spending much of her time sculpting in the basement while her father, willingly, did the shopping and cooking. In fact he celebrated his wife's independence. "Your mother," he told Luree, "is coming into full bloom." Her mother learned to drive in her sixties and propelled "her snappy little 1954 Ford sports coupe . . . up and down the steep hills of Seattle at such a clip" that the family feared for her life.

Luree's aunt, for whom she was named, was still riding in rodeos, on the Appaloosa horses she had broken, in her sixties. When she was seventy she made the National Appaloosa Club's ride of one hundred miles. Luree's grandmother, at ninety, rode one of Aunt Luree's horses. She took her first plane ride at eighty-two, having survived her husband by fifty years, and her daughter and her two sons. Luree wrote of those strong, determined women in her family: "We endure."

The tragedy of that sentence (an echo of Dilsey's last line in Faulkner's *The Sound and the Fury*) lies in the comparatively early death of Luree herself. She too had led an active life. In her sixties she went white-watering with her husband on the Yukon. After his death, she traveled widely in difficult, obscure places like Kazakhstan and Tadzhikistan, about which she wrote a fascinating travel piece for the *Washington Post*.

On her seventieth birthday, ill and weak, she traveled to Costa Rica to visit a friend who had been a member of the first women's team to climb Annapurna. They hiked the rugged terrain of the country. She came back very tired but still fighting her illness with all the force of a tiger. But she did not endure very long.

The account I had read in typescript, I later found out from her son Scott, was the introduction to Luree Miller's book *Late Bloomers* published only in England by the Paddington Press, a good, small press which, I believe, did not last very long. The book was, as the title indicates, about the women who began active careers in their later years after long lives of domesticity and family service. "They are finding it is never too late to seek a newer world," she wrote. Luree died at seventy, having led a brave, adventurous life as long as she could.

◆

ONE EVENING, when I wanted to distract myself from my usual pre-party concerns, I went to a lower shelf in my study where I kept my little collection of E. B. White's books. I found that the edges of the dust jackets of three of the volumes had been chewed by a mouse, but the covers and the texts were intact. I thought White would have enjoyed the knowledge that of all the books in my study—certainly more than a thousand volumes—the visiting rodent had chosen the paper around *his* books to consume. The mouse, I decided, was hungry for fine writing and was making his masticating way toward the pages. I looked at the shelf containing my own books: they had not been disturbed. I considered this choice of White's work by the avid house mouse an act of literary criticism.

White is the most comforting, mind-easing writer I know. He wrote about ordinary subjects in plain but extraordinary prose. One of my favorite pieces is about his return to his house on Allen Cove in Maine, a lovely place on the water where he lived for almost thirty years. It is about eight miles from Sargentville. White set out to answer something the critic Bernard DeVoto had written in *Harper's* magazine shortly before his death. DeVoto disliked U.S. 1, in 1955 the main road into the state. It was "a slum," he claimed, a strip, a sorry mess, ugly. He used what White called another objectionable four-letter word: "neon."

Not so, said White in his gentle rebuttal. To him (and to me forty-five years later) the route has its share of unpleasant but useful modernity but it is "a mixed dish" . . . "the fussy facade of a motor court right next door to the pure geometry of an early nineteenth-century clapboard house with barn attached," although, wryly he admitted "you can certainly learn to spell 'moccasin' while driving into Maine." But when snow fell, "the worst mistakes of men" were erased, covered over and softened. Then, U.S. 1 was "crowned with a cold, inexpensive glory that DeVoto unhappily did not live to see."

How right White was about what, most of all, made the so-called strip acceptable. "Probably a man's destination . . . colors the highway, enlarges or diminishes its defects." He suggested that DeVoto was probably on his way to make a speech or get a degree. White's own "critical faculties," on the other hand, were held in abeyance by the fact that he was heading home.

Coming closer to home, he described driving across the Narramissic, the little river (now a stream), and into and through the village of Orland as he turned off U.S. 1 and headed toward the east. On the road to Brooklin he said he had "the sensation of having received a gift from a true love," and he wittily quoted a poem by a schoolboy who wrote of the river: "It flows through Orland every day."

"Familiarity is the thing—the sense of belonging. It grants exemption from all evil, all shabbiness." In the early evening in winter "the homing traveler" saw the yellow lights in houses along the way, and White, "the soft-minded motorist," had "a sense of perfect security . . . of a just and lasting peace."

I found myself quoting these phrases here rather than paraphrasing them, because when I read E. B. White they remained in my mind: the inexpensive glory of the snow cover and the exemption from seeing shabbiness on the way home.

At the start of his essay White recalled a time when the chimney in his Maine house caught fire. He went into the telephone closet to call the fire department. He explained that the Whites kept their phone in a closet "as you might confine a puppy that isn't fully house-trained." He mourned the advent of the dial system. He would like to have the telephone company shut up in a closet "for having saddled us with dials and deprived us of our beloved operators, who used to know where everybody was, and just what to do about everything including chimney fires."

After he made his dial call in the closet, the fire went out by

itself. He called to cancel the first call. The firemen came anyway, for purely social reasons: "everyone was glad to see everyone else." . . . What a marvelous raconteur. I regret that he is
not here to record the small details of how we now live up here.
I regret that we no longer shut up our telephones in closets. I
regret the loss of operators, together with even the dial system.
We are now at the mercy of buttons that rarely make contact
with a living person. To call beyond Sargentville we need to
know eleven numbers, not the name ("Lucille?" "Muriel?") of
our friendly, well-informed local operator.

I loved reading E. B. White again, for his elegant prose, and
because his recollections of familiar things were my recollections and my familiar things. What is more, I'm glad to be able
to adapt his schoolboy's poetic line for my own purpose: "The
cove outside my window is there every day."

◆

PLACES IN my past have a permanence in my memory that
present change cannot disturb. I will always remember the
fourth floor of the English-Philosophy Building, suite #436, on
the campus of the University of Iowa, the old residence of the
Iowa Writers' Workshop. It has recently been moved to Dey
House on North Clinton Street, a handsome and ample place
near the president's house, I am told.

But set solidly in my memory forever is that old, cramped,
colorless space, a "lounge" with space for five or six students to
sit (although about sixty were enrolled in the program), a rail-
road flat–like series of tiny rooms that served as offices for staff
and faculty (one student, one faculty member, a desk, and two
chairs filled the room), two somewhat larger rooms for meetings furnished with tables and camp chairs, and the sacred hall,
a tiny wall space where six shelves (I think) held copies of stories

and poems "put up" for reading and then harsh criticism at Tuesday meetings of the workshops.

It was a narrow, somewhat mean area, inadequate in every way, and yet, in my time, out of it came extraordinary work and unique writers. It was a limited but (to me) magical place where, for two years, talented people shouldered each other for room and notice, and from which came, in due time, notable novels and volumes of poetry, some of which had been conceived during the workshop meetings.

I have not seen the new location. I refuse to allow it to displace in my mind the long, confined hall off which I worked for three separate semesters and where I encountered students who filled me with awe.

The same set-in-stone permanentization took place in my mind for the building on Q Street in Washington, D.C., that once housed the national offices of Phi Beta Kappa. For six years as a senator (as we were somewhat ostentatiously called) of that august fraternity, I walked to the elegant, white-stone building from the hotel, waited to be buzzed in, climbed the fine winding staircase, and sat in wide, leather-upholstered chairs for long mornings and afternoons of debate on scholarly and administrative matters. It was a large book-lined and paneled room, filled with the cool air of judicious and usually decorous discourse.

Now PBK has moved its quarters to the third floor of an historic building. I have not been there. I suspect it is because, to my way of thinking, the professorial senators are still meeting in the stone building on Q Street, and will be there, forever.

◆

READING PSALMS yesterday morning—at four—I wondered again at the sureness with which the poet addresses his

God, even when He hides from him, refusing to make His presence known. I thought of Proust's words, which I found in Edmund White's new, succinct biography:

> Yet the more one is religious the less one dares to move toward certainty, to go beyond what one actually believes. I don't deny anything, I believe in the possibility of everything.

I recalled Beckett's remark that "the most real element in the fiction you write will be the uncertainty."

◆

FIVE YEARS ago, the librarian in the Ellsworth Public Library sent me a little stack of Library of Congress cards with holes at the center bottom for insertion into the rod of a card catalog. I came upon them yesterday while cleaning a shelf, accompanied by a note. The librarian said they were changing over to an automated system. She thought I might like to have the cards representing every subject in my last memoir, that were no longer of use to them.

What was I to do with the eight tan cards, familiar to me from sixty years of thumbing through similar ones in my search for a book in libraries in many cities and universities? I mourned their passing, remembering my searches in those light-oak drawers. I would rest the drawers on the low, pullout oak shelves while my fingers moved slowly through them. It was far more satisfying (and often more informative) than sitting inert and bleary-eyed before a screen.

But there was more. On an accompanying card, the librarian suggested I should send them off "to my friends and neighbors" saying (I reproduce the suggestion exactly), "Hi, hello, how are ya, I'm fine. By the way, I got my book published. . . ." The thought of doing this was even more shocking to me than the abandonment of card catalogs for computer terminals. The librarian assumed I would celebrate the arrival of the age of technology in the library and the loss of cabinets full of those long drawers, and, what was worse, that I belonged to the new age of self-promotion and would welcome the suggestion that I would "push" my book upon my friends and neighbors. I recalled that even well-known writers, driven by desire for notice that does not diminish as their fame increases, do this sort of thing. Recently, a friend sent me a handsome, hand-drawn postcard, announcing that a story of his would appear in the next issue of *The New Yorker*. Dutifully, I looked for it. It was not there. But it *did* appear in the following issue. The effect of the postcard was somewhat dulled by delay and my surprise at his need for self-promotion.

I threw out the librarian's note, but I saved the cards as mementos of slower, kinder, better times.

◆

I BEGAN TO worry about mosquitoes in the tent. We decided to buy citronella sticks to ward against them. We agreed we were lucky the season for black flies, those miserable insects that fill the air in late May and June and bite without mercy, had passed. This led to ruminations about cluster flies that are cold-weather afflictions. They come into the house around windows, seeking warmth, and then spread out at night to lamps and ceilings. I thought they were rather like human beings, living in tight warm little social groups until the window cooled at night, and then fleeing to the warmer climes (Florida?) of night-light and lamp.

◆

For bedtime reading, having finished the sixth volume of *Remembrance of Things Past,* "The Captive," and eager for some amusement I turned to the letters between Nancy Mitford and Evelyn Waugh. I was doing well with them, laughing at their amusing snobbery and insulting references to their close acquaintances, literary friends, and relatives, until I came upon Waugh's nasty comments on Proust:

> I am reading Proust for the first time—in English of course —and am surprised to find him a mental defective. No one warned me of that. He has absolutely no sense of time. He can't remember anyone's age. In the same summer as Gilberte gives him a marble & Francoise takes him to the public lavatory in the Champs-Elysées, Bloch takes him to a brothel. And as for the jokes—the boredom of Bloch and Cottard.

Waugh was taking to task the great contemporary master of time past, time present, time remembered, time to come, he who saw no real barrier between them all. And did he think he had been promised jokes in the great epic? Nor was he promised careful time sequences (although I suspected Waugh had got it wrong somehow). Proust wanted to explore the results of conjured-up time as a result of the advent of some physical object: the madeleine, the hawthorn bush. A mental defective? Never, no, never, as W. S. Sullivan had written in *Pinafore.*

For me the odd thing was that both Proust and Waugh were great admirers of John Ruskin, a view I have never been able to understand, ever since I was required to read *The Stones of Venice* for an aesthetics course in college and *Sesame and Lilies* at the same time for some other course (I cannot imagine what it might have been). Perhaps I should go back and try Ruskin again. I might now, after the ameliorating influence of sixty-three years, be better able to absorb his complex, thick, and what I remember to be colorless prose.

I finished the letters at midnight and put the thick book down on the floor, trapping the cat's tail briefly between its pages. She gave a critical yip, retrieved her enormous plume, and went angrily away. She has never learned to meow, her greatest virtue to my mind. She remains a silent companion to an almost silent mistress.

Eugene Montale wrote that "the deeper truth belongs to the man who is silent." It would be nice to think so. I doubted it was very often true of me. More often my silence was weariness, or lack of anything significant to say, or laziness. To harbor an occasional "deeper truth" in my quiet state was devoutly to be wished.

◆

"Yet another memoir?" a friend wrote to me when I told him I would have a copy of *The Presence of Absence* for him at the party. This set me back. Why do I go on mining the past, rehearsing it, taking it out and turning it over for endless inspection as though it were a pearl I had uncovered from a just-opened oyster? I thought about Mrs. Dalloway's old friend Peter, coming out of Regent's Park, and thinking about "the compensations for growing old . . . the passions remain as strong as ever, but one has gained, at last, the power which adds the supreme flavour to existence,—the power of taking hold of experience, of turning it round, slowly, in the light." That was what I was doing, turning experience around slowly in the light in yet another memoir, the one about to appear and, oddly enough, about my experience with prayer.

◆

YESTERDAY WAS very warm. I began to worry about the temperature under the tent, having finally managed to dispel my concern about swarms of mosquitoes afflicting my guests. It was noon. I came in from the disturbingly hot deck and sat down at the computer, calling up the file marked "HABIT 3," the novel I had been working on intermittently for twenty years. One time I thought I had finished it and sent it off to Faith Sale, the eminent editor at Putnam who had line-edited an earlier novel. She promptly sent it back, saying that it had too many characters; she couldn't tell one nun from another, she complained.

Obediently, I set out to cut away some of my beloved holy ladies, a jarring enterprise because they all seemed necessary, indeed essential, to the whole scheme: a re-creation of the revolutionary years, for religion, after Vatican II and Pope John XXIII. Now I was back at that book again, despite Sybil's designation of it as the stablemate for the nine books that had surpassed it on their way to publication. Still, I harbored an inexplicable fondness for it, the way a parent must feel for a backward child among a slew of normal ones.

But to my surprise I discovered that, after those decades of disregard, I had developed a dislike of the characters that remained in *The Habit*. How could this have happened? Was it like a biographer's growing aversion to a subject, having learned more and more about her? Or was there a natural hatred that resulted from having once unsuccessfully consigned those people to the page? Or could it be that I had been unjust to them when I saved them from the scissors (an instrument once used on manuscripts before the days of ControlG), only to leave them languishing, undeveloped, on the yellowing sheets of typing paper? Was it guilt for this long neglect that I felt?

Whatever. I went back to work, attempting to portray them

in a better light, trying to make them rounder and somehow deeper on the page, to make them once again the objects of my fictional affection.

When I had finished a few pages it was late afternoon. It had cooled off. I was relieved, having been reminded that it *always* cooled off near the water on July evenings. The temperature in the tent was saved.

◆

My FORMER husband, who has remained a good friend, would not be at the party. His wife was ill, on oxygen constantly, and unable to travel. Leonard too was suffering from a number of somewhat disabling afflictions, but he was caring for her devotedly, overseeing her myriad medications, and doing the household chores. He is a man who has always felt responsible for the welfare of others—for his parents, his daughters, for me when we lived together for thirty-one years. Now he is old, ailing, frail, but still a caretaker.

Over the twenty-five years we have been apart we sometimes talked by telephone, usually on the occasion of a birthday or his hospitalization for a bad heart, or my case of shingles. I consulted him about the efficacy of one medicine or another: he had spent his earlier scholarly life doing research on the analgesic effects of compounds designed by a drug company. When I called to ask him about the lingering pain of post-herpetic neuralgia he gave me a very long, learned lecture about how drugs worked, and then sent me a copy of a paper he had written years ago, which I thought I remembered had something to do with the development of Demerol. I had been using morphine patches for my affliction; he had worked for years on the effects of morphine on pain.

The paper was too dense for my non-scientific mind, but I

was grateful to him for his concern. It had always been this way with him. I remembered one summer when he and his wife, Jane, came to visit a daughter and her family in Maine. Jane and I were swimmers. We headed out together into the Atlantic while he, fearful of the water and our direction, walked up and down the shore, gesturing to us both to come back—

—and I remembered his care for his father, Harry, whose age and loss of any work to do had left him bereft of purpose. Leonard, with the help of his brother-in-law, set him up in a small knitting-goods store in the town of Hazleton, Pennsylvania. At the age of ninety-three Harry was still seated behind the counter, selling yarn to the ladies of the city, advising them on patterns and stitches. On Saturday afternoons a group of young girls would come to the back of his store, where he held classes in knitting. Once, with great pleasure, he reported to me that the previous week a little boy had come by for lessons—

—I remembered Leonard's great concern for his daughters when they were ill. He always stopped their roughnecking for fear they would be hurt. He was a history buff and often drove them out to walk a battlefield in upstate New York. He was not even offended when they preferred to stay in the back of the station wagon reading their comic books.

I remembered the story the obstetrician told me about the birth of our fourth daughter. The doctor went into the waiting room, where my husband was seated reading a scientific journal. "It's another girl," he told him. Leonard looked up and said "That's great," thanked him, and went back to reading his article. He loved having daughters.

In the midst of all the approaching confusion, I hope I remember to call him.

◆

WAITING FOR Sybil to close the bookstore at five o'clock the other day I picked up a mystery by Michael Innis, and read enough to see that *The Daffodil Affair* was about a multiple-personality heroine named Lucy. Such characters seemed to fascinate writers: I recall a book on the best-seller list at one time called *Sybil* about just such a person. Every now and then there appears a semi-scholarly news story about a criminal (always a woman, it seems) whose defense is that she possesses twelve or so personalities, one of which is murderous.

I left Lucy on the bookstore shelf, but I went on thinking about the phenomenon. Isn't it true that we are all Lucys and Sybils, conglomerates of many persons, most of them private, hidden, and disguised—the frightened self, the envious, untidy, ambitious, egotistic, selfish, greedy, distrustful, cold-hearted selves, and the visible, public persons—honest, kindly, humorous, good-natured, self-deprecating, lovable. None of these is dominant, no one adjective could wholly describe the person. All of them are separate entities, warring for control, in one person.

Perhaps this is why some biographers have so much trouble bringing to life on the page the subjects who were complex enough to command their attention in the first place. Or more likely, researchers originally thought their subjects one person, the well-known public one, when they started their work, only, to their dismay, to find they had to deal with all the others.

In my long life I have known a great many people, but very few of them well. Of those I have lived with for a long time, it was most true: they have hidden much of their private selves, for protection, or out of shame, or guilt, or doubt. And the others, those at a distance whom I now called by the more accurate word, "acquaintances," will always be hidden from me because I failed to take the time to know them better.

◆

It is a given: as one ages one seems to lose words, the right word, the *mot juste*, the exact designation that one is searching for. This was true last evening when I went back to *The Habit* to try to rearrange a complex sentence so that it would make simple, direct sense and still convey a complicated idea. The key to this act of illumination, the one word I needed, would not come.

I sat away from the desk to think about this sad diminution of vocabulary in old age. My solution to this plain fact has been to learn *new* words as I read. For example, I am now in possession of "gormless," "phatic," "orts," and "moise," which Jim Crace used in his fine novel, *Arcadia*, that I read recently.

Sadly, I do not believe that I will often need any one of these words. Still . . . I now know that "gormless" is Scots or North British dialect for "gaumless," meaning stupid or dull, a good word but hardly meaningful to an American reader should I choose to use it. "Orts" is better, because crossword-puzzle makers have chosen it for a four-letter word for remains of food from a meal. But the figurative meaning of "to make orts of," that is, to undervalue: I don't know if that would ever be useful.

Further, consider "moise." It too is a late-eighteenth-century dialectic verb meaning to thrive, to mend, to increase. Unfortunately "to moise on the Internet" would puzzle every non-Scots reader. As for "phatic," it has slowly entered the American vocabulary. It denotes speech that is used to express an atmosphere of shared feeling, I learn from the dictionary. Feeling, that is, but not information, which, these days, is called for more often than emotion.

Definitions for "ort," "moise," and "gormless/gaumless" came to me from the *Oxford English Dictionary*. I am the fortunate owner of the sixteen-volume edition, hefty, lovely books, each weighing close to five pounds. Only the bottom shelves of my bookcase can hold these books and, as it happens, I now find it very hard to lift one out and up to the desk.

None of these new (to me) words appear in the more easily accessible *Random House Dictionary of the English Language*, which is mounted on a stand but does not descend to words from North British dialect. So I am destined to learn words, say, from the new translation of Proust: "costive," "quarterings," "muniments," "tergiversations," "cogenes," "autochthonous," "buccal," "crapulous," and others. They will all be useful to me someday, I'm sure, but none of them is as pleasing to the tongue and ear as "moise."

◆

THE ARCHITECTURE of Swedish-built bookshelves is such that the top ones are relatively short. On the other hand, books in our time continue to grow fatter. My habit, after I had, with much effort and arduous bending, returned a volume of the *OED* to its bottom shelf, was to look up to the small shelves in search of some relief. Thus I have re-scanned the three little (six and one half inches high) volumes of *The Anatomy of Melancholy* from the York Library, published in England by George Bell in 1904. The print is very small, the space between lines almost nonexistent but, oh, the little well-bound volumes can be held in one arthritic hand while I try to make my way through the jungle of Robert Burton's sentences.

A more readable book, the two-volume set of Boswell's *Life of Doctor Johnson*, sits beside the *Anatomy*. It's the common Everyman edition, published in 1906, compact, short (seven inches), and printed well enough to encourage browsing. . . . Next I took down C. S. Lewis' *A Preface to Paradise Lost*, a short, elegant essay on Milton's epic poem, published by Oxford in a most acceptable size (seven and a quarter inches high). Because of its insights and finely wrought sentences, I have often thought it more accessible, in one sense, then the poem itself.

In 1980 I acquired Douglas Sutherland's very witty *The English Gentleman's Child*, published by Viking in a narrow (four and three quarter inches wide) volume that still fits the short shelf at eight inches high. Its seventy-six pages are enough (with many drawings) to convey the curious and stringent and funny (to us) life of such a child through to his years in public school. It contains just enough pages to cover the subject wittily and fully, a limitation usually ignored in our logorrheic times.

In 1974 the Hogarth Press published Edwin Muir's *The Structure of the Novel* in a lovely blue-cloth short volume, a little more than seven and a half inches high. I must confess I do not agree with much that Muir has to say about the subject, but it fits well with other books, like Leon Edel's study, *Literary Biography*, which appeared more than forty years ago and is still relevant and useful. Rupert Hart-Davies published it; my copy has the added virtue of being inscribed by the author to "Miss Edith Lewis," the longtime companion of Willa Cather.

. . . And like *Books and the Quiet Life*, by George Gissing, a prize of a little book, of the size (six and three quarters high by four inches wide) that its publisher, Thomas B. Moser of Portland, Maine, used for almost all his books. It was limited to less than a thousand copies. I have the pleasure of owning one of them. It takes up almost no space on the shelf and it remains in my mind as a good study of why one reads.

And Aldine House's very small (four by six) publication in 1906 of Edmund Burke's *Speeches on America*, which boasts a thin, faded red ribbon to keep one's place (why did this amenity disappear from bookmaking except for the Library of America editions?). I cherish my copy, which once belonged to a Miss Downie, who left in its pages the slip that admitted her to a class in Beaver College, Tuesday and Friday, January 4 and 7, in the year 1915.

Miss Downie bought it in a nearby bookstore named (properly) Reeder's in Beaver Falls, Pennsylvania. (The store's little sticker is on the inside back cover). She probably read it to the end because all the pages are cut except the last blank ones. I liked knowing the provenance of a book I owned, valueless (to me) as the book itself may be. I envisioned Miss Downie seated under a tree on the grass in front of her dormitory, reading Burke's close argument against his country's treatment of the colonies, and marking the more debatable points with the red ribbon, perhaps between the pages where I found it. In deference to Miss Downie, I have been careful to leave it there.

Thirty-nine small books fill that shelf. They are reminders of another time, the early years of the twentieth century, when hardback books were often hand- or pocket-sized, when thought was considered valuable when it was condensed into fewer sentences contained on fewer pages, and the price was low. The English publications cost about ten shillings, Miss Downie paid $1.95 for hers.

◆

AN ARTICLE in the local paper, from the Associated Press, the other day took me back fifty years. The headline was "JAPANESE SUBTITLE WRITER'S PEN IS SWORD." "Subtitle?" Was the Japanese woman in the picture doing what I had done briefly in my youth? It turned out to be so. But the story of what she actually did stunned me. Natsuko Toda wrote movie subtitles for major American motion pictures, starting with *Apocalypse Now*, because the people of her country hate movies that are dubbed. Astonishingly, she has attained great power over the films. "When she deems it necessary, she tosses out jokes and sticks in her own. She cuts. She pastes."

Recently she has performed this major surgery on the dialogue in *Titanic, Saving Private Ryan, The Thin Red Line*, and *Shakespeare in Love*. She sees her work as an act of creation. "You are always condensing, cutting, omitting, deciding which part you should put in the subtitle." The only limitation upon her work was the size of the screen, mostly two lines to a subtitle.

Well. I did this kind of work on MGM pictures in New York for the company my uncle owned, Loews Inc. Having the job was a pure matter of nepotism, I'm sure, and I kept it a short time. I was very bad at it. I remember the limitations on the process. There was no creative part. We each had a small machine called a tachistoscope. On it we mounted a reel of the picture we were working on and moved it, frame by frame. Together with the written script, we tried to figure out how much of the dialogue would fit into the frames. It was mainly a matter of condensation, fitting the subtitle to the spoken words.

It was hard. I never really got the hang of it, the way the others at work on tachistoscopes did. (I remember especially a brilliant girl just out of Vassar named Felicia Lamport who went on to write four or five extremely funny books of verse.) Ruefully I remember my worst mistake. I was subtitling an unmemorable film called *Red Rust* with Clark Gable and Jean Harlow. At one point Harlow was taking a soapy bath in a barrel (I believe).

Some of her décolletage showed above the bubbles, but I, fool that I was, considered the dialogue more important and imposed four lines of talk on the few frames, thus covering what was, my boss informed me, what the viewers in South America were most interested in.

I argued that it was a plot point, that it required all those lines. He looked at me as though I had lost my mind, and soon afterward I lost my job. So Miss Toda's freedom to write whatever she wished: add, cut, invent, all these free activities struck me as highly desirable. If it had been part of the allowable procedure in my time, I might have succeeded better. I might have been better at the creative part that Miss Toda talked about and have written subtitles that bore only a token resemblance to the story. I might even have invented a few jokes to brighten up the dreary story. My pen might have been a sword and I would have become, as the article reports of Miss Toda, "one of the most powerful people in the movie industry." Oh well.

◆

OVER AND over again I walked the stretch of lawn on which the tent was going to be placed. I was certain it would not fit. The huge rock that occupied the center of the space would interfere with it. There was no way it would work. I communicated this new worry to the caterer when, at last, he came by for final instructions (I had begun to convince myself that he had moved away without informing me). "Don't give it a thought," he said in what I considered an offhand manner.

I went in to my swivel chair in the morning to make a note on the list of worries. On the little table beside the chair is a high cup that held a variety of pens. When I wrote in my notebook, I liked to have a choice. One, with a felt tip, wrote softly

and was suitable for more elevated thoughts, like John San-
ford's perspicacious remark, "The Law was a protection against
the direct experience of God." I had intended to use it in the
book about private prayer, but somehow missed it. So it remained in my notebook, lightly put down as from a great distance.

Another pen had a black, free-flowing tip that I used when I
was angry or objected fiercely to something, such as, "HOW
DOES HE KNOW FOR SURE IT WILL FIT?" A third made a thin,
hard line that was suited to matters so personal that I knew I
would never use them but I could not resist the temptation to
write about them, discreetly.

I chose the one that suited my level of gravity, and could then
tell at a glance, by the character of the ink, which entry in my
notebook did. This variety of penmanship was impossible
when one wrote on a word processor. The printout always
looked the same: gray and indifferent.

◆

KITTY KELLEY sat with her back to me. I called her name.
She turned her head to look at me. It appeared she finally knew
her name. I felt honored.

◆

IN THE evening, after my final pacing of the lawn, I sat on the
deck and waited for the streetlight at the end of the point of the
cove to come on. There was no reason for the light, no one lived
down there except in "the season," and the road to the two
summer houses ended there. I may have been the only person
to whom that streetlight was meaningful. When it grew very

dark, working on some sort of sensor system, it came on, and then went off at dawn.

Now it grew very dark, the light came on. It seemed to me that the greater the darkness the smaller the light. Yet it was there. I thought: no darkness was ever complete, for the light, or something lighter than darkness, was there to define it, to make it *visible*. There was always something to mark its blackness. Just so, no silence was absolute without a sound, no matter how distant or tiny, to make one aware of it, to make it *heard*.

I went on sitting in the almost-dark of the deck, thinking about-to-be eighty, on the cusp of the End, close to the ultimate Darkness and Silence. Perhaps the condition of dying would be like this: a mysterious and microscopic light in the infinite darkness, a pygmy sound in the vast silence.

◆

In THIS summer of political scandal in Washington, I often thought of my acquaintance, I. F. Stone, with whom I shared an office almost twenty years ago at American University. Sybil reported that customers asked regularly to buy his signed photograph, which hangs in the bookstore. She would not part with it at any price. And I wished he were alive and still writing his *Weekly* because he would have made wonderful sense of party hatreds and the disappointing president's personal mistakes, even stupidities.

Izzy Stone was offered a desk and an office by the chairman of the English department. He needed a place to work on his translation of Plato's *The Republic*. He had given up his influential letter from Washington to study the politics of the fourth century B.C. because he thought the existing translations misinterpreted Plato. He was seventy-two years old, his vision was very bad, but he had just begun to teach himself Greek. I was many years away from having known the language. Together we puzzled out a few sections of *Oedipus Rex*.

Why Sophocles? It was practice for him; he thought it would be better to learn the language using the short lines of drama before he started on political philosophy. In time, he mastered Attic Greek well enough to write and have his book published.

I remembered he once quoted Albert Camus to me: "There is no truth, only truths." He lived his extraordinary intellectual life by that dictum. I wished he were still around to translate some of the current complex Washington deceptions into simple truths. I wanted to look at his photograph again so I went to the bookstore to look at it.

"We see only what we look for in need," said Roger Fry of an artwork, I believe.

◆

To FILL an afternoon before the first guest, my daughter from New York, arrived, I thought it might be interesting to me to gather the statistics for the year of my birth. From six or seven sources, I learned that it had been a terrible year in which to be born, a year marked primarily by death: worldwide, almost 22 million persons died of what was called the "Spanish influenza."

Half a million of these were Americans. My mother was fortunate: half of those who died in Manhattan, where we lived, were pregnant women. She and I survived. In the same month, the entire royal Russian Romanov family was shot to death.

It was the last year of World War I. Ten million persons were lost in that conflict; 20 million were blinded, crippled, shell-shocked, or otherwise disabled. The poet Wilfred Owen died on the battlefield at the age of twenty-five, two days before the

Armistice. It seemed significant to me that the horse that won
the Kentucky Derby that year was named Exterminator.

Woodrow Wilson was president. Englishwomen were
granted the right to vote as a result of their active participation
in the war and the rigorous campaign led by Emmeline Pank-
hurst and other suffragettes.

In that year Houghton Mifflin published Willa Cather's *My
Antonia* in a press run of two thousand copies. The favorite toy
for Christmas 1918 was the Raggedy Ann doll, and in the fall
Congress passed the Daylight Savings law. The Red Sox won
the World Series against the Chicago Cubs; Charles Birdseye
began to freeze vegetables.

Eighty years ago the favorite stars of motion pictures were
Mary Pickford, Douglas Fairbanks, Charlie Chaplin, Theda
Bara, Mabel Norman, and Constance Talmadge. Postage
stamps could be purchased for three cents, a quart of milk was
thirteen, a pound loaf of bread was ten cents. You could buy a
house for a little under five thousand dollars.

In 1918, Ella Fitzgerald, Mickey Spillane, Ingmar Bergman,
Spiro Agnew, and Ted Williams were born. Two of them, I be-
lieve, are gone, and Spiro Agnew, Ted Williams, and Ingmar
Bergman, I believe, are still here.

In her novel *Dolly*, Anita Brookner wrote, "The look that is
cast back falsifies." Perhaps so. But these facts seemed hard and
fast. It may be that my choice of them, out of the thousands of
other available "facts," is false. I thought I might read these statistics aloud during some lull in the serving of dinner, perhaps
while the lobsters were being dismantled.

◆

On my small shelf I came upon a curiosity, Hans Kung, the
great Catholic theologian, writing on Mozart. I opened to a

page on which he said that a musical work is not finished when it is written down, or even when it is performed, but only when it is heard. I thought it might be the same with a poem or a novel. They were completed, not when they are abandoned by the writer, and not when they are put into print and arrive at the bookstore, but when they are read or heard. . . . And similarly, the liturgies of the church, codified in millions of leaflets, missals, books of common prayer, and other official prayer books, do not exist, indeed, have no reality until the worshiper, in church or outside, gives them life through prayer, thus *finishing* them.

Those who pray may carry this even further, believing that no prayer is complete until God hears (and who knows when and if this occurs) and responds, or does not, if He chooses not to. Only then is ritual prayer complete. Who knows? Knows God, as Henry Luce would have put it in old *Time* style.

◆

TRYING ON new clothes that I had ordered from catalogs for the event, I was reminded yet once again of the sorry state of my body, the inevitable decline of its parts, the sagging of its once firm flesh, the loss of shape of thighs and buttocks and breasts that accompanies being eighty. I only knew one person who had been able to take this condition with any degree of humor: Betty Comden.

I came upon her, and her book, *Off Stage*, four years ago at a book and author luncheon in Detroit. But we first met sixty years ago in the ladies' room at Washington Square College in Greenwich Village. She was at the mirror, her head tilted back as she meticulously and heavily applied mascara to her eyelashes. We began to talk about her performance in some play that I had seen, a production by the Washington Square Players. It was a time when I was divided between my studies in philosophy and my teenaged infatuation with the theater. I was awestruck by actresses and thought her very glamorous.

I never encountered her again at the college, but my husband and I saw her in many performances of a group called the Revuers who appeared at Café Society Downtown (I think it was). It was a witty musical group of four who did skits and songs: the others were Lenny (then called) Bernstein, Judy Holiday, and Betty's partner-to-be, Adolph Green.

Sixty years later I arrived at the hotel where the luncheon was to be held and immediately asked if Betty Comden was there yet. "Oh yes, she is," the chairman said. "She's in the ladies' room." And there she was, standing at the mirror, looking almost as glamorous as I remembered, reinforcing her eyelashes with heavy mascara. I decided that she had never been far from a mirror in her life and the results justified the means.

I took home a copy of her book. On the flyleaf inscription she promised to give me "an eye-make-up lesson" anytime I said. No such occasion arose, but when I felt particularly downcast about how I had come to look, I reread parts of *Off Stage*, especially her honest descriptions of her lifelong absorption with her looks. She wrote that, when she decided to go on the stage, she had her nose "fixed." The pictures in the book testify that she continued to look quite beautiful into her eighties, but her essay called "My Body Revisited" brought her to my position on old age, except that, by some miracle, she surveyed her state with her usual good humor.

She wrote that she hated the "appellation senior citizen" and could only come up with "time-challenged." "It tells you that here is someone who is still a viable human being, capable despite some rotten thing that happened [the passing of the years], something beyond that person's control." And, after a spurt of her gaiety ("Am I not determined to do great in spite of it? Ha, ha. Time, I challenge you!") she asked herself: "Is it now OK to cut the euphemisms, face the facts, and use the word *old?*" No, she declared, "not yet." Wittily, she paraphrased Eliot: "I grow time-challenged. I grow time-challenged. I shall wear the bottom of my blue-jeans rolled."

Even after mourning the loss of her crowning glory, "fat" hair, she accommodated to it with frivolous bangs that also hide the furrows between her brows. Then there is the thinning of her eyebrows ("Is it plain balding?"), which an eyebrow pencil takes care of, and all the eye operations and transplants her endothelial dystrophy has required, leaving her not seeing very well, in her phrase. Add some "lingering arthritis in arms and hands"—to which she responded "but I do not care to give it the time of day"—and "a mitral valve prolapse somewhere in the heart, but they keep telling me it's nothing, so I'll tell you it's nothing."

So it goes on, making the wry best of everything, shaming me for my usual dour outlook on old age. However, the best thing in the chapter is her recounting of a story about W. Somerset Maugham, who was asked to give a lecture, "The Beauties and Recompenses of Growing Old." An aged man by then, Maugham came onstage to face an enormous audience, and sat in a chair. "He paused. He stared out at the audience. The pause took on epic proportions. Finally he rose and said, 'I can't think of any,' and walked off the stage."

Betty Comden, that humorous, happy soul, concurred. "I just want to say 'Move over, Willie. I agree with you.'" After that short bow to my pessimism she straightened up and concluded, "Even so, somehow I keep trying to stick to my premise that I have come through many things and will come through a lot more, and although 'time-challenged,' I want to try to be insouciant, optimistic. . . ."

I have not seen her since. She is a year older than I will be next week. I picture her still at some mirror, her makeup intact, and not yet agreeing with that slogan I saw recently on a car bumper:

"Aging is the only way to live."

◆

MARGARET WHALEN's long, commodious house in York Beach had two boarders, sisters who were ninety-four and eighty-seven. They had never liked each other, had not spoken for years, ate their meals and spent their days and nights alone at each end of the house. After the death of the younger, the survivor was entirely indifferent. Their resolve to continue some lifelong feud or dislike might have strengthened their aging. . . . Words fail me.

◆

NEIGHBORS, FRIENDS, family, publishing people, agent, writer-comrades have all departed. Sybil's dinner, to which guests had come from a distance to a local restaurant to drink, eat, toast, and mingle with strangers to them, is over. All our worry about who should sit with whom has been dissipated.

The festivities under the tent next evening, during which guests ate lobsters, corn roasted in its husk, blueberry pie, and drank champagne and wine, a typical Maine dinner to show those from away what we, on occasion, eat here, are concluded.

Two days later the tent was taken down and trucked away. The caterer loaded his car with all the supplementary materials.

Sunday breakfast at Oakland House has been eaten. My son-in-law, whom I have known for thirty years, made the acquaintance of my friend of almost sixty years when we worked together at *Architectural Forum*. He promises to bring her fresh leeks from his garden in upstate New York. All the cars (which found adequate parking spaces that evening without any trouble) and the planes have gone.

Sybil and I sit on the deck, looking out at the cove, studying the grass on the lawn now a little less green where the tent stood, a slightly yellowed reminder of the good company that had assembled there.

This is the summer of my unexpected content.

◆

I HAVE BEGUN to reread Proust.

◆

I AM ON another cycle of praying the Psalms in the perfect silence of the morning room at 5 A.M. within sight of a red sky and dark water.

◆

IN MY notebook I have written that the great painter Renoir, his paintbrush strapped to his crippled right hand, said: "You don't need your hand to paint."

◆

HAVING READ T. S. Eliot, Doris Lessing, and best of all, Leonard Michaels' sentences about his cat ("People wonder

how a cat resembles them psychologically. A cat wonders similarly about people," and "The silence of a cat makes the world
unreal") I have vowed not to write a book about our cat.

◆

In a very real way, I find that I am still living with my dead
friends.

◆

The party is over.